Also from GHF Press

Making the Choice
When Typical School Doesn't Fit Your Atypical Child

Forging Paths
Beyond Traditional Schooling

If This is a Gift, Can I Send it Back?
Surviving in the Land of the Gifted and Twice Exceptional

Learning in the 21st Century
How to Connect, Collaborate, and Create

How to Work and Homeschool
Practical Tips, Advice, and Strategies from Parents

Educating Your Gifted Child
How One Public School Teacher Embraced Homeschooling

Self-Directed Learning
Documentation and Life Stories

Gifted, Bullied, Resilient
A Brief Guide for Smart Families

Writing Your Own Script:

A Parent's Role in the Gifted Child's Social Development

By Corin Barsily Goodwin
&
Mika Gustavson

Edited by Sarah J. Wilson

Published by GHF Press
A Division of Gifted Homeschoolers Forum
3701 Pacific Ave. SE - PMB #609
Olympia, WA 98501

ISBN-13: 978-0692524343 (GHF Press)
ISBN-10: 0692524347

Cover design by Shawn Keehne.
www.shawnkeehne.com • skeehne@mac.com

Dedication

To Madeline & Benjamin, who set me on this path, and to Robert, who supports me in ways I have never before been supported. I love you all. ~CBG

This one's for Rich and Seth—thanks for being on this wild ride together! ~MG

Contents

Acknowledgments

Nothing I write would be complete without a nod to my co-author, Mika Gustavson, with whom I share a neural connection, and Sarah Wilson, who is endlessly patient while herding our work to completion by any means necessary. Thanks also to the GHF board, staff, and the entire community of wonderful people who give me hope for humanity. Thanks, also, to Chester, who supervised. (No cats were harmed in the writing of this book. Don't believe a word he says.) ~CBG

Huge thanks to my co-author, Corin Barsily Goodwin, whose seemingly innocent comments like "We should write a book about that!" have once again landed us here. I'm also grateful to Sarah Wilson, our editrice extraordinaire, without whom our sentences would have been so much longer. Thanks also to the entire GHF family, for existing, and to coffee, for always being there to perk me up. ~MG

Introduction

Over the years, you may have worried whether your child's friendships were sufficient, or noticed that she seemed to have few friends, or wondered why it seemed so difficult for her to make and maintain friendships. Your child might have required more assistance with interactions because when left to her own devices she seemed to be lonely, fodder for bullies, or at a loss for how to interact appropriately. Perhaps you thought you would send your child out the door and she would automatically fit into the neighborhood crowd, or that she would make bosom buddies with her classmates. Maybe you hoped that building friendships would come naturally, "just like everyone else."

Along with your concerns about how your child was doing socially, you may also have asked *why* the interpersonal experiences are so different for your child, and what you may have done (or failed to do) as a parent that contributed to a less-than-ideal social landscape for your child. It turns out that many gifted and twice-exceptional (2e) kids need a different approach socially, just as they need different approaches for learning. As with the other aspects of these kiddos' lives, we parents need to learn to make up our own script, rather than follow the pathways set up for more typical families. So many people have lots of apparently great advice, but what works for—or looks like a problem for—others may not hold true for our children.

So, what is a parent to do? Information goes a long way toward easing your own anxiety and being better able to help your child find the relationships he wants or needs. Unfortunately, most of the books available on friendships do not take into account giftedness as a social-emotional factor. Some books may even address aspects of giftedness or other neurological differences, but most do not discuss in-depth the role of parents in their kids' friendships. That is what drove us to write this book.

As you read this book, it is important to retain a clear sense of the difference between what we want for our children, what our agenda is, and what our children may want for themselves. As adults, we may have a better grasp of the possibilities and might see opportunities which our children are unaware of, but frequently our own need or desire for our children to meet our expectations socially is at least as much of a problem as our children's quirkiness, intensity, or outlier status.

It is more than all right for our kids to be who they are. We should celebrate their "differentness" rather than merely tolerate it. Still, their differentness may make it difficult for them to find close friends, a community, and the sense of belonging that, as human beings, we all crave. It also makes parenting them more challenging, although the payoffs are tremendous and the costs of doing otherwise are significant.

For some of you, this may be relatively new territory. We have included a significant amount of background information in the first chapter for those of you who are just beginning in the world of gifted. If you've been hanging out at this party for a while, feel free to skip ahead. We hope this will make our book useful no matter where you are in your journey.

Prologue
Pre-Production

How is a parent to know what is enough and what is too much? What is helpful and what is interference? One guideline we frequently turn to is our favorite definition of the role of a parent, coined by Mica Fuller, MFT:

> *The role of a parent is to create an environment that is safe, structured, and supportive, in which a child can explore, make decisions, make mistakes, and self-correct in order to become an independent and self-sufficient adult.*

This powerful guideline scales and adapts to whatever your child needs. Of course, what makes an environment "safe, structured, and supportive" will vary according to your child's specific age and developmental needs and challenges. What you need to do as a parent at park day when your child is having a "hard day" and few true peers are present, for example, may be entirely different than when your child is having an "easy day" with a one-on-one "sure shelter" type interaction. The level of intervention required of you will likely also shift with increasing levels of familiarity with a certain environment, as well as whenever there is a change in that environment, such as a new student in a class or a field-trip outside the familiar frame of the class.

This definition also articulates and recognizes the normalcy of making mistakes as a part of a child's development. The process of learning is articulated as a four-step process: exploration, decision-making, mistake-making, and self-correction. If we regard the mistake step as an error, a wrong turn, we are unnecessarily judging the experience as a failure, as well as truncating the learning process and impeding its positive trajectory. This scenario plays out frequently in group settings, such as a classroom or park day, when conflict occurs between two or more children. The supervising adults see this as bad, a sign that something is wrong and that should not have happened. Parents frequently experience consternation, even leading to parallel conflict between them, in an effort to resolve or avoid conflict at all costs. This misses the point of the interaction for the children, the very thing from which they are most likely to benefit. If they are protected or prevented from experiencing the conflict (otherwise known as the "mistake" step), they will not ever get to the integration of new behaviors (otherwise known as the "self-correct" step).

Now, this in no way means that when your child is caught up in a conflict (or especially a pattern of conflicts) that you should stand back and let him deal with it unsupported (see the first part of the definition). However, using this model as a guideline, you can navigate the pathway and strike a balance between providing support which is sufficient for your child, but does not actually prevent the learning process from unfolding. Also, it can be infinitely reassuring to know that *you* do not need to panic when your child makes a mistake.

This four-step process of learning appears as though it should unfold naturally if we parents provide the environment and stay out of the way. For some children, this is how it works. For others, especially those who are twice-exceptional, it may be necessary to guide them explicitly through the steps—another reason this definition rocks: It gives parents a blueprint for how they might help their children move through the social learning process.

Chapter One

Backdrop: What You Should Know About the Gifted Child

Giftedness is not merely a cognitive construct. Some people equate the term "gifted" with talent or achievement or eminence or good grades in school. Other well-respected experts prefer a different perspective—one not limited to a view of giftedness as what a person can produce—which is the understanding that we will use here. Most parents of gifted children come to the realization fairly early on that something about their children is *different*, and they usually figure that out long before the kids are able to sit in an elementary school classroom. Whether it is early alertness, extreme intensity, or asynchronous developmental milestones, young gifted children often stand out among their age peers.

Of course, *all* children are unique individuals. Much of what we have to say about gifted kids will apply to all children to some extent. What is significant is in the magnitude of difference between gifted and everyone else. While the needs of gifted kids might significantly overlap those of neurotypical kids much of the time, the differences are thrown into high relief when considering social issues. Outlier kids have greater hurdles to jump, and, thus, so do their parents.

While gifted kids are all different from each other, and parents may not need or want to follow the same steps for each child, we can make some generalizations to assist in better understanding the unique individuals whom we are privileged to parent. Some of what we discuss will resonate with you; some may not. You are the expert on your child. Take whatever is helpful.

Who is the Gifted Child?

In the last 20 or so years, much has been written to help parents and educators understand what qualities and characteristics are common among gifted children. A quick internet search of "gifted characteristics" reveals nearly thirteen billion hits. Many lists overlap significantly, although a skeptical eye might notice that each list will have its own biases and highlights.

Dr. Linda Silverman of the Gifted Development Center has developed a testing instrument called the Characteristics of Giftedness Scale. Her list includes the following:

- Reasons well (good thinker)
- Learns rapidly
- Has extensive vocabulary
- Has an excellent memory
- Has a long attention span (if interested)
- Sensitive (feelings hurt easily)
- Shows compassion
- Perfectionistic
- Intense
- Morally sensitive
- Has strong curiosity
- Perseverant in their interests
- Has high degree of energy
- Prefers older companions or adults
- Has a wide range of interests

- Has a great sense of humor

- Early or avid reader (if too young to read, loves being read to)

- Concerned with justice, fairness

- Judgment mature for age (at times)

- Is a keen observer

- Has a vivid imagination

- Is highly creative

- Tends to question authority

- Has facility with numbers

- Good at jigsaw puzzles

It should, of course, be noted that these are guidelines: a greater proportion of gifted children have these traits than would be predicted in the general population. Keep in mind, though, that just because your child only matches a few of these traits does not mean she is not gifted. It may simply mean that her giftedness manifests somewhat differently or possibly is camouflaged by other issues. Research shows that parental observations are the best predictors of giftedness in children.

In spite of our ability to make lists of characteristics and global features of "giftedness," a very important factor is at play as well: gifted children are all different from each other. No single framework can or will ever define the social needs for every gifted child. Like all children, gifted children have a need for friends and social interactions, but their needs are all over the map.

The challenge here is that gifted children are much more complex and may require a different and more creative or persistent approach than that of neurotypical kids. Some of the threads that need to be woven together in order to create such an approach include asynchronous development, twice-exceptionality, overexcitabilites, emotional maturity, temperament, and unusual interests. We will discuss each of these, and explore how they may impact your child's ability to form satisfying social connections.

Asynchronous Development

You will often hear parents complain about how their 10-year-old child does high school level academics, plays soccer like a seven-year-old, occasionally spouts the wisdom of a much older person, yet has the hissy fits of a two-year-old. This is asynchrony (uneven development) in action. The term "asynchronous development" describes what happens when a child's brain "comes online" in an order significantly different from the accepted norm. This can manifest in a variety of ways, including uneven skills acquisition, missed or advanced developmental milestones, or a significant disparity between what they know and what they can demonstrate. These children are often misjudged and assumed to be immature or oversensitive. People also often assume the worst of asynchronous children, believing that if a child has difficulties in one area, then she should be held to that place across the board (e.g., *If you can't read this book without crying, maybe you shouldn't be reading such advanced material at all.*). Alternatively, people may assume these children intentionally misbehave or are lazy (e.g., *If you're so smart, why can't you . . . ?*). In fact, consistency is not a strength of asynchronous development. A child may have all of the stars aligned to complete a task one day, but the next day she is tired or anxious or focused on something else and cannot quite get it together the way she did before.

But, how does this relate to friendships? Having a friend who can meet you at your developmental level, make the same intellectual leaps, understand your jokes, and share interests matters a lot. So it becomes important to consider placing an asynchronous child with their academic peers for learning activities, even though he may still continue to need support and scaffolding. In addition, they may actually need another group of peers; one based on shared interests, rather than strictly an academic situation. Just as many adults find themselves with one set of friends for a particular activity and a different set for another, complex asynchronous children can also benefit from such an arrangement.

One young lady we know has excelled as a young college student, graduating with honors at 17 years old, but in preparing to go off to graduate school she inquired about social opportunities on campus with the undergraduate population with whom she is likely to have more in common in terms of life experience. On the other end of the childhood timeline, consider the three-year-old whose speech patterns are commensurate with his age. While he tries to assist older children with an engineering project they are having difficulty with, even though he is clearly way ahead of them in knowledge and could be helpful, they will not listen to him because he "talks like a baby."

Other examples of asynchronies creating a barrier to social connections include:

- The adolescent taking a literature class which includes topics that tweak his emotional sensitivity

- The teen participating in a chemistry lab who has fine-motor trouble handling the equipment

- A tween who excels in her high school level debate club, but gets treated like the little sister instead of a peer

- The early college student who has plenty of acquaintances on the college campus but cannot date or go out with her friends because she is underage

- The preschooler who would rather spend time with the adults because the other kids are "boring"

- The school-aged child who wants to hang out with the neighborhood kids but has not yet mastered riding a bike to keep up with them

- The little girl who wants to play "house" with all of the other kids, but her version of the game includes far more detailed accuracy than theirs (e.g., hand-washing pioneer doll clothes in a puddle out back), so the other kids get bored and walk away

- The preteen who enjoys playing Magic: The Gathering with an older crowd, but melts down when he loses a match and is unable to compromise on minor issues, insisting on putting being "right" ahead of the social relationship

An additional note: Emotional maturity varies between individuals and excessive emotional sensitivity may be mistaken as a lack of maturity. Sensitivity is part of who a person is and how he feels in the world, while maturity—including the skills to deal with big feelings appropriately—comes with time and effort. The sensitive seven-year-old may burst into tears at the plight of the homeless person sitting on the curb, yet she may also be the leader in a group of children who organizes a fundraising effort to help the local homeless shelter. The tears are part of her sensitivity, but her ability and willingness to understand and take action regarding these feelings involves a higher level of maturity. As she gets older and develops more maturity, the tearful outbursts will likely be replaced with other behaviors more suitable to the social context.

Twice-exceptionalities

Most gifted children are developmentally asynchronous, but when the unevenness in their abilities is significant these children are considered "twice exceptional" or "2e." This means the child is both gifted and has identified learning differences or other emotional or mental health disorders, which can include ADD/ADHD, autism spectrum disorders, OCD, anxiety disorders, or sensory, auditory, and visual processing disorders, as well as dyslexia and dysgraphia, among others. Gifted children may have sufficiently intense overexcitabilities (explained in the next section) so as to create obstacles for them in living and learning. Children who are twice exceptional are often misdiagnosed or one of their diagnoses is overlooked by the adults around them. Consequently, many 2e children are not identified until they score a wide spread in intelligence assessment subtests. An example of this misunderstanding comes from one youngster we know who had difficulties with gross motor development—the sort of thing that is necessary for running, climbing and other typical activities of four- to five-year-old boys. His lagging development in this area was missed because whenever his preschool teachers encouraged him to go play on the monkey bars or run around on the playground, he would employ his highly precocious verbal abilities, and charm the teachers with a "No, thank you, I don't care for that," which was so cute they forgot to notice that he was not actually able to do the things he was being asked to do.

Twice-exceptional children will also be able to compensate for an area of weakness by using their advanced cognitive abilities. This can result in a child who puts a tremendous amount of effort into or is abnormally tired from participating in social interactions. When a child compensates like this, she reaches a point where she crashes and burns. Year by year, the demands increase, and she can only compensate for so long. Moreover, she is undoubtedly aware that she is working harder than she "should" have to, which impacts her self-image and self-esteem. Twice-exceptional children commonly assume that the way they experience the world is the same as everyone else, and since they are struggling and the other children appear not to be, something is wrong with them. When such a scenario happens over and over to a child who already seems qualitatively different, the effect may reinforce her sense of isolation, loneliness, and poor self-esteem.

Other examples of twice-exceptionality creating a barrier to social connections include:

- The child with social difficulties who expends great amounts of effort in order to function, and when she runs out, she is just *done*. A playdate may be bubbling along until, suddenly and strangely (from the parents' perspective), it is a disaster and one of the children is melting down or insisting it is time to leave *right now*. Frequently, observers call this behavior "rude" or "manipulative." In reality, the child ran out of emotional resources because the supposedly "easy challenge" of playing at someone else's house was actually a very significant stretch.

- The child with an auditory processing disorder whose language instructor insists she is making excuses, when in fact she is working doubly hard to comprehend what is being said.

- The child who does get accommodations for his developmental disability, but is seen by other children as getting special privileges. Adults set the tone for other children, who pick up the attitude and integrate it into their view of the 2e child.

- The girl who enjoys sharing her enthusiasm on a favorite topic but is seen by others as "weird," "arrogant," or "conceited," rather than smart. This becomes a bigger issue when her second exceptionality includes behaviors or manifestations that make her appear visibly different, such as idiosyncrasies of speech (pauses, fillers, frequent sighs, or flat tones). This unusual delivery can be distracting and interfere with the listener's ability to focus on the content of her communication.

- The boy who has behavioral asynchronies or "stims" (self-stimulatory behavior), such as moving around a setting, incessant tapping, rocking, head banging, tapping, humming, or interrupting, that lead others to assume he is not very intelligent. When he makes a joke that goes over the head of his age peers, the others assume the problem lies with the joker rather than the audience. Instead of the boy telling himself, "Oh, my joke went over their heads," the label of "weird" is reflected back at him creating more negative self-views.

Intensity and Dabrowski's Overexcitabilities (OEs)

In the world of giftedness, "intense" is probably the most agreed-upon term to describe children like ours. It is also probably one of the most misunderstood aspects of giftedness, giving rise to comments like "Chill out. It's just not that important." But for these children, it actually *is* that important. By dismissing the level of intensity the child is expressing, we send a potentially damaging message: *the way they see and live in the world is incorrect or wrong.*

Beyond the damage this dismissal can do to interpersonal relationships, the denial of their authentic experience sets the scene for children to question and double-check their interpretation of events. They may to learn to "dumb down" or hold back who they really are for fear of rejection or ridicule. While modulating how much intensity one shows is certainly an important social skill, an across-the-board message that intensity is bad can be crippling.

In fact, this intensity is part and parcel of the gifted experience. One framework which helps us to understand intensity in gifted individuals was conceived by Kazimierz Dabrowski (1902-1980), a Polish psychologist, psychiatrist, and physician. He coined the term "overexcitability," or OE (or also translated "superstimulatability"), to describe five attributes frequently observed in the gifted. These attributes are not always about loud, big, or fast. If we think of overexcitabilities as a description of the "text" of a gifted child's life, then "intensity" describes the delivery of the text. Gifted children may shout, whisper, intone, or chant "To be or not to be," but they will likely never deliver it flat. Some parents will say that intensity does not describe their child because their child seems so self-contained, not recognizing that intensity can just as easily be quiet as loud.

While not all gifted individuals have OEs, many do, and frequently they have more than one. Much has been written about OEs; author Stephanie Tolan, co-author of *Guiding the Gifted Child*, characterizes them as "[five] areas a person reacts more strongly than normal for a longer period than normal to a stimulus that may be very small. It involves not just psychological factors but central nervous system sensitivity."[1]

OEs are divided into psychomotor, sensual, imaginational, intellectual, and emotional, all with positive and negative aspects.

Psychomotor OE

The child with Psychomotor OE needs to be moving in order for their brain to be engaged. If you have ever sat in a meeting with a person who fidgets constantly with her pen or has her leg moving or foot tapping all the time, that is an adult with Psychomotor OE who has learned to channel it in socially appropriate ways. For children, the positive aspects of Psychomotor OE frequently include plenty of energy, enthusiasm, and stamina for a variety of activities. The downside, of course, can be that the need for movement is at odds with behavioral expectations in a given setting. In fact, this OE is frequently misdiagnosed as an attentional disorder such as ADHD.

Dr. James Webb, in his book *Searching for Meaning: Idealism, Bright Minds, Disillusionment, and Hope,* explains that the child with Psychomotor Overexcitability, when emotionally tense, may:

> . . . *talk compulsively, act impulsively, display nervous habits, show intense drive, compulsively organize, become extremely competitive, or engage in adrenaline-stimulating behaviors. Their activity can be overwhelming; some of these individuals never seem to sit still. People around them may want to tell them to please sit down and be quiet!* [2]

Some examples of Psychomotor OE impacting social interactions include:

- The tween boy who attends a scout meeting and spends the entire time wiggling in his seat, tapping the side of his chair, or otherwise disturbing the other children

- The little girl who loves historical documentaries and brings her dolls to act out scenarios while she watches. This cements her learning but distracts anyone watching with her

Sensual OE

Sensual OE includes both the "sensory" issues (for example, tags in shirts, sensitivity to smells, dislike of certain food textures) and a profound response to sensory input. If your child is moved to tears by a sunset, or "eats his food with his eyes" before chowing down, he may have this OE. People with this OE may react negatively to sounds most people can barely hear or the barely-perceptible blinking of fluorescent lights in a classroom. They are also likely to have an increased and early appreciation of aesthetic pleasures such as music, language, and art, getting absorbed in a particular song or painting. Sensual OE may contribute in some ways to the development of addictions, as the receptivity to the stimulation of some drugs and alcohol can be heightened. Puberty may result in risky sexual behavior among those children who exhibit sensual overexcitability. Participation in social events may also be limited by a negative response to the smell, noise, and feel of crowds. Both Psychomotor and Sensual overexcitabilities may play a part in insomnia among some gifted individuals.

Some examples of Sensual OE in social dynamics include:

- The teenager who cries over poetry and gets marginalized by his age peers

- The girl who copes with feelings of otherness by plugging into her iPod and letting the music soothe her, not realizing that this actually increases her isolation

- The young foodie who enjoys the taste, smell, and texture of food so much that health concerns arise

- The child who declines invitations to birthday parties or attends them but hides in a corner to avoid the auditory and visual overstimulation inherent in these events

Imaginational OE

Children with Imaginational OE sometimes blend reality and fantasy because their new ideas get mixed together in their minds or because they simply enjoy their own internal world more than the external world. They become emotionally invested in the stories they create, often preferring their imaginary experiences to the comparative blandness or, in some cases, threatening experiences of everyday reality. The child with Imaginational OE finds the creativity of developing stories in his head far more compelling than the repetitiveness of a traditional curriculum. Many children with Imaginational OE enjoy writing fiction or poetry. Others express these tendencies through their artwork, their Lego creations, or even in intuitive leaps leading to scientific breakthroughs. Imaginary friends of all kinds abound, each with their own carefully crafted and detailed back story.

Understand that children with Imaginational OE do not fail to recognize the difference between their imaginary life and "real" life; rather, they tend to hold them as equally important to each other, and frequently expect everyone else to have the same standard. This can cause conflict or confusion when others fail to do so.

Some examples of Imaginational OE in social settings or relationships include:

- The young girl with an extensive family of dolls and stuffed animals, who expected her human family to know and respect the doll family's relationships and dynamics, up to and including birthdays and other celebrations

- The nine-year-old boy with an imaginary friend who was a brilliant physicist with whom he enjoyed discussing such concepts as the nature of the universe

- The four-year-old girl who had a very real relationship with an invisible pet pterodactyl and would sometimes become upset and intractable if the adults in her life failed to treat her imaginary friend as real; buckling her into her car seat got quite complicated, as the pterodactyl also needed to be safely restrained in his own seat for the car ride

Intellectual OE

Children with Intellectual OE often fit the stereotype of "gifted" in the academic sense. They frequently do well in school and enjoy more traditional forms of learning; but, this love of intellectual stimulation can sometimes cause difficulties for the student in a classroom situation. For example, when a teacher needs to move from one subject to the next, a child with Intellectual OE may want to keep going deeper into the first subject, or share a great deal of information on the topic that he has gleefully researched on his own, resulting in a mismatch which can lead to distress and discord.

Additionally, children with Intellectual OE often have problems with boredom beyond the typical "I'm bored" attitude we all experience at some point. Their brains need such a high level or great breadth of stimulation that the lack of either leads to behavioral issues. Moreover, these kids may not be clear that this is what is happening. The inability to understand and articulate their own needs is particularly problematic when adults who do not understand giftedness or OEs hold the child to a high behavioral standard while unintentionally stinting on the feeding of her brain. While all children need intellectual stimulation, gifted children with Intellectual OE often need a level beyond what the adults around them realize is necessary. As part of this required stimulation, these kids have a tendency to "overintellectualize" ideas by launching into a detailed discussion or thoughtful monologue on a concept that others do not feel is worth the time.

Consider the situation with a fifth grade girl who was so taken by a class discussion of Egyptian mythology that she steeped herself in everything on the topic that the internet had to offer. By the following day, she was prepared to discuss what she had learned and was dismayed and frustrated that the class was moving on to some other aspects of Egyptian culture. Moreover, the teacher was none too pleased by the fact that this student now knew more about Egyptian myths than he did. When she (accurately and politely) corrected the teacher in front of the class, the teacher declared her wrong and sent her to the principal. That negative experience sent a message to the girl that her interests did not matter and, that by extension, she did not matter because nobody wanted to hear what she had to say.

Some other examples of Intellectual OE impacting social relationships include:

- The preschooler who wants nothing more than to discuss higher mathematical concepts with his playmates who have barely learned to recognize their numbers

- The young teen in a college class who wants to be included socially but cannot seem to stop herself from bringing up complex concepts in class that will not be on the test, simply because she finds the subject fascinating

- The tween boy who over-thinks what others say and how they react to him, reading more into their behavior than is actually going on, often assuming negatives where there are none

Emotional OE

For a child with Emotional OE, every day is either "The best day of my life!" or "The worst day, *ever*," or even both, depending on when you ask. Additionally, Emotional OE can lead to problems with managing emotional states and recognizing those of others, including difficulty distinguishing the boundary between other's feelings and one's own. This tendency to reflect the emotions of others can lead to spiraling interactions, where if one person is irritated, the other reflects it back, and so on, potentially eroding the goodwill in the relationship.

One challenging aspect of Emotional OE in both parenting and social relationships is the frequent experience of interacting with a child who has been overwrought but is now ready to move on, while the other party is still reeling from the onslaught of emotion they were subjected to. Few children will continue to do the work involved in maintaining a friendship with another child who drains them or frustrates them in this manner. It becomes significantly worse when *everyone* involved has this OE. Their intensities bounce off of each other to the detriment of the relationship, making it hard to find ways to restore balance and equanimity.

Some of the ways Emotional OE can manifest include:

- A thirteen-year-old girl who, distraught because a friend "snubbed" her in the hallway at school, becomes anxious and distracted, only to find later the friend had had earphones in and did not actually see her

- A four-year-old boy bursts into tears when his playmate falls and scrapes his knee

- A ten-year-old girl who clings to her mother in an attempt to shield herself from all the mixed feelings she perceives at a family gathering

While not every gifted child has all of the overexcitabilities, when they do have them, they usually have more than one. This leads to the overexcitabilities getting mashed together, making it hard to distinguish which one you are seeing at any given moment. Additionally, since all children change and develop throughout their childhood, it can be difficult to distinguish developmental challenges from OE issues. For example, one boy was held back in kindergarten because "he spent last year crying too much and needs time to mature," when, in fact, he was bored with the oversimplified lessons. He had taught himself to read fluently at age three and highly valued accurate information (Intellectual OE). He was frustrated with the other children who wanted to play dress-up but were unwilling to let him "correct" historically inaccurate costuming details (Imaginational OE). He did not understand why they did not share his interests or value his opinions, and it bothered him that they were often changing stories and getting details wrong in their play. His confusion and lack of scaffolding from the adults led him to believe that something was wrong with him and become especially sensitive to perceived slights, which led him to become upset and cry frequently (Emotional OE). When viewed through the lens of multiple overexcitabilities, this situation becomes more complex, requiring a nuanced set of responses from the adults who were likely unaware of the depth of the drama playing out in the social interactions among the children.

Introversion and Extraversion

Common wisdom has long held that the gifted population has a preponderance of introverts. Whether or not this is true, what really matters is that you acknowledge your child's temperament and work with it respectfully. Encouraging an extravert to sit quietly with a book all day long, day after day, is likely to lead to frustration for both the child and the parent, while pushing an introvert to be a social butterfly and expressing disappointment when he is not the center of a lively social group is setting everyone up for failure. As parents, we need to drop any expectations of who our children should be and consider who they actually are.

Books such as *Quiet: The Power of Introverts in a World that Can't Stop Talking*, by Susan Cain, or *The Introvert Advantage: How to Thrive in an Extrovert World*, by Marti Olsen Laney, have addressed the challenges of being oneself in a society that seems to hold extroversion up as the norm while pathologizing introversion. Susan Cain writes:

> Introverts . . . *may have strong social skills and enjoy parties and business meetings, but after a while wish they were home in their pajamas. They prefer to devote their social energies to close friends, colleagues, and family. They listen more than they talk, think before they speak, and often feel as if they express themselves better in writing than in conversation. They tend to dislike conflict. Many have a horror of small talk, but enjoy deep discussions.*[3]

So what are introversion and extraversion, anyway? According to the Meyers-Briggs Foundation, which represents the founders of the personality measurement movement that gave us the terms:

- Everyone spends some time extraverting and some time introverting. Do not confuse introversion with shyness or reclusiveness. They are not related.

- Extraverts often like getting energy from active involvement in events and having a lot of different activities. They are excited when around people and enjoy energizing others. They like moving into action and making things happen. Extraverts generally feel at home in the world, and often understand a problem better when they can hear what others have to say.

- Introverts like getting their energy from dealing with the ideas, pictures, memories, and reactions that are inside their head, in their inner world. They often prefer doing things alone or with one or two people they feel comfortable with. Ideas are as important as activities. Sometimes they like the idea of something better than the real thing.

Adapted from *Looking at Type: The Fundamentals*, by Charles R. Martin[4]

In fact, recent research seems to indicate that extraversion and introversion are correlated to quantifiable brain differences. As author Ben Thomas states in his article for the Crux blog, "Are the Brains of Introverts and Extroverts Actually Different?," "[A]lthough the science of personality is still in the relative Dark Ages, researchers have begun to draw links between what these structural and functional brain differences between personality types might mean in terms of their respective peccadilloes." He goes on to remind the reader of the importance of not conflating correlation with causation, as we certainly have yet to figure out if those brain differences come about because of temperament, or whether they cause temperament (or some other as-yet-undiscovered third option).[5] Evidence indicates that temperament is an actual *thing*, not merely a proto-scientific concept.

That said, temperament is not necessarily a fixed nor binary entity. One can be strongly or weakly introverted, and that movement along the continuum is normal across a lifespan. Indeed, a new term, "ambivert," has been coined to describe those who move from one side to the other, depending on their preference and situation.

The point we are making here is that much of our society is set up to encourage and even glorify extraverted traits, regardless of the actual temperament of the individual. For example, we often push children out onto the playground when they may rather stay inside and read a book, or insist they join in a group game and not be "unfriendly" or "stuck up" when their preference may be to walk alone and think or decompress from being around other people for too long. We tease them about not being social butterflies and comment on how they "don't have enough friends to make a birthday party" when they are quite satisfied with their one or two close friends. One girl we know had a huge seventh birthday party, and afterward her mother told her how nice it was to have so many friends to share it with. The little girl replied that it was fun and she had enjoyed the party, but for the next year she preferred to spend more time with the people she really liked and fewer playdates with the rest of them. The following year, she celebrated her birthday at a tea house with just a few friends—a tremendous success.

As a parent, the trick is recognizing that although your child's preferences and ways of being in the world may be different from yours, they are valid and appropriate for the child, and there is nothing wrong with the child who chooses the opposite of what you would. This can be challenging, however, when you have to find the right balance for multiple preferences in one family. While adults can be more flexible than children (for example, an introverted mom can bring a book to park day and let her child run around among friends, or she can allow her child to bring a book or other activity along for those times when he needs to retreat), families with more than one child and one flavor of social need may need to try different options in order to determine what works for them.

One of the joys of parenting is learning about yourself through acknowledging your child's needs, thus gaining self-validation and perspective. An interesting phenomenon of parental self-discovery is the significant number of parents of gifted children who report having learned (or been trained) to present as the opposite of their natural tendency. For much of their lives they believed that were one type, only to discover the opposite trait stronger within them.

Ultimately, what you need to do is to take seriously your child's presentation of temperament, and adjust your expectations based on that. You will need to develop plans and activities which, especially in the beginnings of social relationships, leverage the areas where your child is most at ease. If it is very important to you (or to your child) to push his limits out further, do so gradually and not at a time and place where doing so would be unnecessarily stressful or have negative social consequences.

Unusual Interests

In the world of social connections, your gifted child will more likely find a true peer among other gifted kids. But the mere fact of giftedness is not sufficient in and of itself. Being gifted does not necessarily equate to shared interests or levels of intensity. Although common membership in a high IQ group could, in fact, be a pool for possible friendships, having similar numbers in common is not what creates bonds, but the ability to "get" each other. If you have one child who is intensely interested in the finer details of medieval weaponry, one who is obsessed with the relationship between hem lengths and the economy, one who cares deeply about maritime exploration technology, and another who wants to talk about Pokémon all day long, those children are unlikely to be a good fit for close friendship with each other. That said, those kids who recognize "same otherness" in another gifted child may build completely unexpected friendships based not on shared activities or interests, but on their mutual desire for connection.

Parents often worry that their children's unusual interests mean they will never find others who share their passions. What these parents need to remember is that that gifted kids are kids, and they may move on to other obsessions (eventually) or find others online (thank goodness for the internet!) who share those interests. Parents might also consider bringing the child to the interest, such as making a trip to MineCon or a fiber fair or enrolling their child in an advanced course in geospatial mapping.

A joke often shared in the gifted community goes as follows:

> Child: "Mom, when am I going to find other people who like the same stuff?"
>
> Mom: "Don't worry honey, there is a time and place for that."
>
> Child: "When?"
>
> Mom: "Grad school."

Of course, grad school is not the only way (or only time) a child or young adult will find her people. But the joke does shine a light on the fact that there is a world of difference between the options available to children and young adults who still need the support and scaffolding of their parental home and relationships, and the options available to independent and self-sufficient adults.

Struggling to help your child find friends can be demoralizing when his interests seem so esoteric—and let's face it, those esoteric interests are sometimes the very things that seem to keep him from connecting with others, even other gifted kids. Parents must dredge up the ability to hold down negative reactions to the "weirdness" of their child's interest, as it will only drive a wedge between you and your child, as well as send the message that something is inherently wrong with him if he has this interest.

What you *can* do is help him find others that share his interest, whether they are same age or not, and help him recognize that his current environment may not be conducive to making those connections. Help your child understand that the problem of finding connections may not lie in your child's differentness but in the place and time that he is seeking those connections. While it would be wonderful to have a close friendship at all stages of life, reality does not always work that way. Most adults have different friends or groups of friends for different interests or activities, and that is an approach that can be effective for our children. It may not be as satisfying as we would like, but in lieu of the close friendship they crave, it may be what is available to them at a given time.

Thinking strategically about factors such as temperament, twice-exceptionality, and unusual interests will allow you to choose situations more likely to be successful for your child but do not require her to stretch in too many different ways simultaneously. Functioning in an appropriately friendly and social way is in and of itself very challenging for a lot of children. Adding in sensory overstimulation, anxiety about location or activity (like swimming or biking or anything that could, for that individual child, present worries), or a general environment that is a bad fit temperamentally (such as a big party for the introvert, or one-on-one in the library for the extravert) is setting her up to fail socially. Once the social groundwork has been laid and a relationship is solid and comfortable to the child, a parent can introduce some of the other challenges. At that point, the friendship can even act as a form of scaffolding to help overcome other issues.

Merely knowing a child is gifted does not give us all the information we need to understand what makes him unique. Knowing a child is gifted *does* help us understand that we are going to have to do more to find friends than simply put him in a group with other smart kids. Having examined the background issues facing gifted children in the social arena, let us now delve into what social connections mean and feel like from the child's perspective.

Chapter Two

Setting the Scene: Friendship and the Gifted Child

As we launch into a discussion of what friendship means to gifted children, we must remember there is a difference between what we observe and what they are feeling. As parents, we have a responsibility to distinguish between what we want and hope for our children, and what they, as their own separate people, actually want or need for themselves. We must walk a fine line between helping our children find their niche and pushing our children into situations for which they are not well-suited and may result in negative consequences.

Developmental Stages of Friendship

Skeptics might wonder why helping gifted kids find friends is such a big deal. As parents, we are often accused of helicopter parenting or being elitist. "How difficult is it to make friends," we are asked. "Why do they need their parents to help them, and why do these friends have to be 'just so'? Won't any other similar-aged kids do?"

Well, no, other age peers may not be a good fit. It depends on the child and, critically, on what kind of friendship she is seeking. A friendship based on parallel or even cooperative play is very different from one that provides the sense of acceptance and belonging that a more mature friendship will bring. In her article, "Play Partner or Sure Shelter? What Gifted Children Look for in Friendship," Dr. Miraca Gross lays out a five-level framework for describing the developmental range of friendships.[6] Her focus was not so much what friendships look like from the outside, but how a child's understanding of what a relationship can be changes over time. The five stages appear from simplest to most complex in terms of age and concept:

- **Stage 1: Play partner**
  In the earliest stage of friendship, the relationship is based on "play-partnership." A friend is seen as someone who engages the child in play and permits him to use or borrow playthings.

- **Stage 2: People to chat to**
  The sharing of interests becomes an important element in friendship choice. Conversations between "friends" are no longer related simply to the game or activity in which the children are directly engaged.

- **Stage 3: Help and encouragement**
  The friend is seen as someone who will offer help, support, or encouragement. However, the advantages of friendship flow in one direction; the child does not yet see himself as having the obligation to provide help or support in return.

- **Stage 4: Intimacy/empathy**
  The child now realizes that in friendship the need and obligation to give comfort and support flows both ways and, indeed, the giving of affection, as well as receiving it, becomes an important element in the relationship. This stage sees a deepening of intimacy, an emotional sharing and bonding.

- **Stage 5: The sure shelter**
  The title comes from a passage in one of the apocryphal books of the Old Testament: "A faithful friend is a sure shelter; whoever finds one has found a rare treasure" (Ecclesiasticus, 6:14). At this stage, friendship is perceived as a deep and lasting relationship of trust, fidelity and unconditional acceptance. As a highly gifted 12-year-old described it:

A real friend is a place you go when you need to take off the masks. You can say what you want to your friend because you know that your friend will really listen and even if he doesn't like what you say, he will still like you. You can take off your camouflage with a real friend and still feel safe.

Dr. Gross also found that gifted children were generally farther along the hierarchy of stages of friendship than their average-ability age-peers. So a child who is yearning for the closeness of a stage four or five friendship ahead of her age peers may not only be unable to satisfy that need, she may also come to wonder if something is wrong with her since the other kids do not want to interact on that level.

The Need to Belong

The need to belong is a subject of considerable study in modern social psychology, and is coming to be identified as a prime component of what makes us human. Dr. Dylan Selterman, in his blog *The Science of Relationships,* mentions the work of psychologists Roy Baumeister and Mark Leary, saying "The 'belongingness hypothesis' states that people have a basic psychological need to feel closely connected to others, and that caring, affectionate bonds from close relationships are a major part of human behavior."[7]

One of the key sources of research which supports the hypothesis is the observation of the consequences of deprivation on individuals. Selterman states, "When people lack meaningful close relationships with others, they suffer. Specifically, married individuals are healthier, less stressed out, and are expected to live longer than single individuals. Close relationships boost people's immune systems."[8] While our children are not married yet, the research on the impact of close relationships easily generalizes to an understanding of how humans are hard-wired for connection from the very start.

As parents of gifted and 2e children, we must figure out how to support our children as they seek to fulfill that need, and our role is a

25

vital part of scaffolding their friendships. Children who are "not like everyone else" need assistance in negotiating relationships for two key reasons. First, this is a numbers game. When you are an outlier in the population, it is just plain difficult to find others who match your quirks and needs. Second, these relationships are more complex due to the disparity in development through the stages of friendship.

If gifted kids did not feel a need to belong, finding a good fit for friendship would be a whole lot easier. But they do need to belong, and we want to help them satisfy that basic human desire. Parents may find it difficult to reassure their children that "nothing is wrong with them" when the need for friendship is not being met. Even a child who appears to have a great number of friendly acquaintances may be lonely in a crowd. The child may desire something that simply is not available from his age-peers. This can also impact the child's self-esteem and lifelong willingness to approach others, especially if he has been rebuffed often or painfully enough. For example, a gifted two-year-old at a kids' playgroup approached several of the other children and tried chatting with them. When the other children looked at her like she was a space alien come to Earth and hid behind their parents' legs, the little girl felt hurt and refused to continue attending the group. As this was a formative experience for her, it created barriers and hesitation in approaching others throughout her childhood. What the girl did not know at the time was that most two-year-olds were at Stage 1 while she was well into Stage 2, seeking someone to chat with. Moreover, the older she got, the greater the disparity, as she blew through the developmental friendship stages much more quickly than the children around her. Not until she had been in college for some time did she finally find intellectual peers interested in closer friendships.

Unfortunately, adolescence may heighten the challenge highly asynchronous children experience in finding friendships. A young teen boy who is both gifted and has social skill delays may find himself among older teens and young adults in an academic setting, perfectly able to hold his own in classroom discussions, but socially isolated because his classmates do not want to hang out after class and obsess about Minecraft, nor are the kids with whom he does his online gaming interested in discussing the similarities in appearance between Minecraft and images from transmission electron microscopy.

Sometimes all that is required to help a child feel that sense of belonging is a parent or other adult modeling appropriate responses or interactions for the other children. In one situation, a young boy's robotics classmates did not understand the content of the advanced references he made to various scientific concepts, so all they paid attention to was his awkward delivery of those comments. The boy felt badly about himself and despaired of ever fitting into the group. Only when the instructor explained the subtlety of the humor did the rest of the class understand that the content of the comments was actually on topic and rather advanced intellectually. While not all of the other kids could relate to this level of sophistication, some of them were finally able to see the individual behind the social quirkiness and the childhood lisp. While close bonding did not happen right away, the isolation lessened and the boy was able to participate in the class without constantly worrying that he would say something "wrong."

Impact of Loneliness and Feeling "Other" on Social Interactions

The discussion of the loneliness of gifted children has been ongoing since the early twentieth century. Seemingly simple solutions often turn out to be anything but. The inherent potential for loneliness when one is an outlier undermines even the best of "friendship making guidelines" for gifted children. After all, if you are one in a million, finding someone else even sort of like you can be an onerous task. Moreover, a friendship connection depends on both people in the relationship. Your child could do everything "right" (however you define "right"), yet the friendship still may not take. As is often said, you can control your own behavior but not that of other people.

The eminent psychiatrist Frieda Fromm-Reichmann once chastised her fellow therapists for withdrawing from emotionally unreachable patients rather than risk being contaminated by them. The uncanny specter of loneliness "touches on our own possibility of loneliness," she said. "We evade it and feel guilty."[9] Therapists are not the only people who withdraw from those who are lonely. Feelings of discomfort are common around people who are lonely—ironic, since those people probably yearn and hope for connection. So a child looking for a friend can be perceived as "trying too hard" or "being too needy," and encounter greater rejection because of her isolation, or subject herself to peer pressure, inappropriate behaviors, or bullying in a "devil's bargain" in order to have friends. Teasing and bullying may only serve to reinforce thoughts of helplessness, defectiveness, vulnerability, failure, or worthlessness. While loneliness and lack of friends are not the same things, adults may be perceived as such and then unintentionally place a child in an inappropriate environment and pressure her to fit in and make friends, whatever it takes.

Psychobiologists have shown that "loneliness sends misleading hormonal signals, rejiggers the molecules on genes that govern behavior, and wrenches a slew of other systems out of whack."[10] We know loneliness is not healthy for adults or children, so parents of gifted children are right to prioritize their efforts to help their children find a good social fit. The fit does not have to be with age peers, nor does it need to be as part of a crowd. It does, however, have to fill the longing for intimate friendship that their child seeks to assuage.

Loneliness is generally understood to be an interior, subjective experience, not an external, objective condition. Still, we feel uncomfortable by the apparent loneliness of others, and as parents we can sometimes mistake our own discomfort with our child's lack of (or minimal amount of) friends for our child's subjective needs—which may not be the same thing. We may also push our children to "go play with the neighbors," not out of a genuine understanding of their social needs, but because of our own desire to have them "fit in" or to be occupied without our needing to participate. As parents, we may really want to believe the common wisdom that if we place our children in a typical childhood setting, "they will be fine." It can be difficult to separate what others say and what we believe to be true. As parents, we don't always trust our own instinct. We should.

Chapter Three
Casting: Finding the Other Players

Who might be a good friend for your child? What are the interests and characteristics of that hypothetical friend? Do friends even have to be other children? Do you need to consider the family (siblings, parents) of the child in question, or the social dynamics of groups of children? You might find yourself hanging out with some of these friends; what would that be like? The answers will vary depending on the age of your child. A young child and a teen will have different needs, issues, and logistical challenges. Clearly, the interplay among developmental factors in friendship, intellect, and emotional maturity must also be considered. When your mother-in-law tells you to just send the child to school, or your ex-husband insists on sending your child out to play and then blames the child for not fitting in, you need to understand, as does your child, that it is not a matter of being too picky or elitist or wrong in any way. A gifted child's not fitting in is a function of having more factors to consider and fewer possibilities to work with. This complexity adds layers of challenge for both children and parents, often leaving children needing parental guidance and parents seeking advice and support from anywhere they can find it.

As we said earlier, since all gifted children are different from each other, offering general or blanket suggestions on how to proceed is difficult. It would be great if we could offer a laundry list, broken down by age group, of places to go and things to try, but you would not need this book if it were that straightforward. Instead, we can offer a list of concrete questions to ask yourself about your child and his needs, and more questions regarding the resources you may have available to you in your community and online, in order for you to generate your own personal list of places to go and things to try in support of your child's social development.

What does my child want? Do I really understand, or am I making assumptions?

First, you must separate out what your child wants from what you think she *should* want. You also need to recognize that what she wanted or was satisfied with six months ago may not be what she is seeking now. Moreover, what she *thinks* she wants may not actually be what makes her feel happy. It may seem obvious, but many parents get into a groove of making assumptions about or decisions for their young child only to miss the developmental shift where their children either became a more articulate advocate for their own preferences or went "underground," putting what they think they are supposed to want ahead of their real desires. Checking in with your child on a regular basis allows you to assure her that she is entitled to have unique needs, and that you are interested in helping her get them met. This is a good first step toward helping her satisfy her friendship needs.

Is what my child says he wants consistent with what I know to be his abilities and limitations and with societal expectations? How can I make these discrepancies less of an issue?

It is not uncommon for what a child wants to be beyond their reach in some areas, but with gifted children the asynchronies can make this situation more dramatic. Accommodating and scaffolding them in order to meet some of their needs and desires helps, but this can be complicated by the confluence of a child's asynchronies and societal expectations. For example, a child may insist he wants to enroll in an advanced math class, yet he is unable to stop talking long enough for the teacher to teach and his endless questions irritate the other students. Accompanying him to a community college class in order to provide subtle guidance on behavioral issues may be acceptable, since the age range in the student population is broad and adults are often students. If, however, this were in a class for younger people, the same accommodation of bringing Mom along would stand out and be viewed as strange. Whatever accommodations you choose should be adapted to the particulars of your situation.

Sometimes, the accommodations are simple and will not impact others all that much. For example, if a child is sensory sensitive, perhaps she can wear earplugs in order to make the desired tap-dancing class work for her. Other accommodations may be less straightforward and depend more on personal interactions. For example, a new boy expecting to make lots of new friends in the homeschool group could find his inability to read social cues a barrier to his goal. Scaffolding this kind of situation directly is difficult, but perhaps a few lessons in spelling out the unwritten rules of social behavior would not go amiss, particularly if the child does not seem to intuit these guidelines on his own. Perhaps reading some of the many books aimed at children and teens on how to interact socially and on the dynamic nature of these issues would prove useful. (See *Resources*.)

Are my child's expectations of social interactions realistic? How are those expectations being formed? Can I help develop a broad and nuanced view of social interactions?

Many gifted and 2e children devour books and movies which show peer (and even child-adult) relationships in an unrealistic light, happy endings and all. The kids in the books may be different or even bullied, but in the end they develop wonderful friendships and all is well. Gifted and 2e kids yearn for those happy endings without necessarily realizing that real life is more complex. Most of these portrayals disproportionately highlight the positive (or simply more exciting) aspects of a situation, while minimizing the boring or painful aspects. Moreover, most forms of media portrayals of society lean toward outrageous outliers, with the goal of creating emotional pull and drawing in an audience wishing to be entertained. One young man we know, as he was contemplating attending a local high school after many years of homeschooling, cited the show *Glee* as his motivation for wanting a traditional high school experience. He said that he wanted all of the singing and camaraderie depicted in the show. He completely overlooked the themes of school bullying, homophobia, and jockeying for popularity that *Glee* also portrays.

Knowing when to talk to your child or show her images of what real life can look like can be hard. Often, kids see only the aspects of relationships that they want to see, or know how to see, creating a challenging parenting situation. For example, what do you do when other kids are making fun of your child and she sees it as "all in good fun"? On the one hand, you do not want to hurt your child with the bad news; on the other hand, recognizing negative intent in another person is a critical life skill. What about the child who is trying hard to compare his own situation with something he read in his favorite book, but it turns out that some critical pieces are missing? Do you point out the missing pieces and sadden your child? Or, do you ignore it and hope for the best? As your child gets older, you may also have to explain that the nice young adult who is paying attention to her does not actually share her passion for Doctor Who, but appears to have a more nefarious purpose. Younger children may want to be helpful in finding the stranger's lost puppy, but they do not understand that they are actually placing themselves in a dangerous situation. These are difficult situations to address. You will want to make certain to consider all of the aspects of each instance, including the following:

- How important is it that your child be "shown the light" right now? Is this a good time to mess with his reality, or should it maybe wait until next time? What are the likely consequences?

- Does your child have low self-esteem? How will an understanding of the harsh reality impact that aspect of your child's development?

- If this is an appropriate or necessary teachable moment, what is the best way to handle it? Are you and your child better off taking a walk in the park to talk, or staying somewhere private?

A child who is likely to fall apart does not need their personal anguish displayed for public consumption.

- Are safety considerations an issue? The nice man at the park feeding the ducks may be one of the few people happy to listen to your child rattle on about her favorite topic, but is he safe?

- What about trust issues? If you do not level with your child, then if he finds out the truth later. he may resent you for, in his mind, allowing him to be teased or humiliated.

Obviously, there is no one-size-fits-all solution. We hope it helps to know that you are not alone, that other parents struggle with the same questions for their own children.

Why is it so hard to find a good social environment for my child?

Finding a perfect setting for more typical children where all their various needs can be met is challenging enough. Searching for that nirvana when your child is an outlier is likely to be an exercise in futility. Better to take as axiomatic that the "perfect" place probably does not exist, and make plans to meet what needs you can while scaffolding the rest. Best practices have long indicated that the most positive outcomes arise when children are placed according to their cognitive level and provided scaffolding in other areas. A child who is very different is not necessarily lacking friends because she is in an advanced classroom or activity; however, she might have difficulty in building satisfying friendships because she is very different. She will almost certainly have the same or similar problems in age-based environments, but at least in more advanced activities she will have some of her needs met, rather than none.

Finding Other Players

As you are looking for venues to find friends and companions for your child, keep in mind that the mindset he has going in will greatly influence the sense of success he associates with the experience. If he approaches it as "I just know I'm going to hate this" or "They will all hate me," he will undoubtedly be correct. If you can guide him towards an attitude of "Cool! I get to do (fill in activity) and I might meet some new people," the outcome will likely be much more satisfying. How to get there will be different for each child, but involves less focus on outcomes and more on the here and now. If the child has had negative experiences trying new things in the past, help him analyze and understand those situations, identify the forks in the road, and determine what, if any, different choices he could have made. After participating in the new activity, reinforce the idea that even if he did not find the best friend he had hoped for, at least he had a good time, got great practice with early stage social skills, and may have made an acquaintance who will later introduce him to that new best friend. At this point in the process, "no effort is wasted" is a good motto.

So where are all those great activities hiding? If you are fortunate enough to live in an area rich with resources, you can reach out to local museums, libraries, hacker spaces, universities, and other amenities. Parks and recreation programs may offer classes, and 4-H or the local school district could have opportunities for learning and socializing. In those cases, you will have to do some research to find the right fit. Do not be afraid to call it quits when something is not working, whether it is expectations, personality, or whatever, even if you have already forked over the money.

In some areas, particularly rural and low income areas, education may not be considered a priority or funding is not available, so it will take a lot more work on your part to create opportunities. You may have to seek out less obvious resources to meet your child's needs. For example, a retiree with an interest in materials science may be willing to share her career experience, or a local artist may be interested in working with a young and enthusiastic learner. Do not despair if you do not find anything right away. Your child's interests may change, or you may discover new prospects as you continue the conversation with the people you encounter.

Perhaps the most difficult part of this for parents is the simple fact that, in order to help your child find friends and acquaintances that meet her needs, *you* must lay the groundwork. That means that you have to be sociable at least enough to discover those community resources. You may, in fact, find it uncomfortable to approach strangers or acquaintances in an attempt to create a network for yourself and your child, or you might personally prefer not to participate as much in a community, but you have to put yourself out there because your child's needs require it. On the bright side, your child will see you modeling the very skills she will need to use herself. As adults, we have developed a variety of coping skills for social situations, some of them conscious and others more automatic. We select them from our "toolbox" in challenging situations. Becoming aware of our own methods is like taking inventory of all the tools in the toolbox. Sharing this inventory with our children gives them the opportunity to learn what is possible and decide which tools may work for them.

You will need to put yourself out there and ask others to spend time with your child, knowing that your child may be difficult to interact with at times. You have to find a balance between asking people to share themselves with your child while you stay out of the way and giving them the information they need in order to understand your child—how he learns and what he needs. You may need to be nearby to intervene in case of a meltdown or to gently guide the new relationship, and this may be required more in some situations than others. You also have to be willing to risk your adult relationships with others who may not only end up disliking your child but blame you for what they see as poor behavior, or view you as "hovering." Stay strong and focused on your child's needs.

Finding Mentors

Adults, young adults, and older youths can be great resources for gifted and 2e children. Many older people are thrilled to pass on their knowledge to the younger generation. Moreover, if their interests are unusual as well, they may be happy to have someone to share them with. Children may prefer practicing relationship skills with an adult who has more maturity, wider experience leading to more social flexibility, and less stringent behavioral expectations. Many adults will have skills or talents that have been long buried under the responsibilities of adulthood; mentoring a young person gives them an opportunity to revisit their lapsed passions.

So, how do you find a mentor?

Identify your goals

Consider why you want a mentor. What you think would be a good fit for your child? Does your child want a mentor? What do you and your child hope to get out of this relationship? Do you want to address a specific topic or are you looking for an adult friend and role model? Do you want someone who can open the door to a field or community? The answers will help you determine your direction (or directions), as one person may serve the role in multiple areas or multiple mentors may be what you need.

You will also want to talk with your child and use some of your own intuition to determine whether someone male or female, young or old, and with particular areas of expertise or skills would fit best. Whatever you decide, do keep an open mind. Do not pass up an otherwise perfect opportunity simply because the right person has the wrong number of X chromosomes!

Do your homework

What groups or communities exist in your area? Is there a 4-H program, a Boys & Girls Club, a hiking meet-up, a gem society, a fiber arts guild? What about cosplay, a library group, or a faith-based organization? If there is nothing local, try online. If your child is interested in edible plants, see if the local park district offers guided walks. Perhaps volunteering at a museum or with a local animal shelter will help your child make contact with others who share her interests. If you cannot find an obvious fit for your child, or your desert community does not have a community ski team, you will have to research further. For example, a college or university in the area may have a youth program, or they may be able to recommend a tutor who can teach your child mathematics while geeking out over Doctor Who and also serving as a social skills role model when she takes your child to play Magic: The Gathering at the gaming club.

Keep in mind that not only do children's interests change over time, but so does the community. Circle back around from time to time to see if anything (or anyone) new has appeared on the horizon.

If you do all of this work and determine that no one within a reasonable distance can fill the role of mentor, you will have to take your research online. Once you reach that level, you can continue searching online for local resources, while looking farther afield. Distance is not necessarily a limiting factor in mentor or any other relationships in our global community. Specialized websites, topical discussion lists, and relevant blogs offer opportunities to interact with experts and enthusiasts, and on the internet, if you ask a good question, nobody knows you are only nine years old.

Reach out and touch someone

Once you have narrowed down your options, make a phone call, send an email, yell across the back fence, or approach a potential mentor or a common acquaintance. Check with local colleges or universities where a professor or an eager student might be available. Some parents will reach out to college departments to inquire about courses their child can sit in on, or students who would like to earn pocket money spending time discussing theoretical physics with a 14-year-old. Others might befriend a professor by inviting them for dinner and conversation.

Using the internet to find local or specific resources is not much different from finding a mentor in person. Email, Skype, and Google Hangouts are all opportunities to appropriately approach and meet with mentors. Contacting someone from out of the blue, even if they are rock-star-famous, is no longer considered impolite. They may not reply to your missives, but then again, they just might. Be polite and recognize that *you* are asking *them* for something, and their time is valuable. You should find a way to make sure the relationship is mutually beneficial, which could mean financial compensation, or simply having a young person who looks up to them and contributes to the discussions. Keep in mind that if your child cannot behave appropriately, do not expect the mentor to waste her time while your child acts out or misbehaves. Consider that your child's acting out may actually be a signal that she is not ready for this relationship or that it is not a good fit. Call it quits when it is time to call it quits. Some mentor relationships will be very brief, while others may last years.

Attend a meeting or event

Rather than seeking out a specific individual with whom to connect, you might take your child to an event that interests him. For example, a stargazing club for the junior astronomer could be a fun way to spend time with your child, let him learn about his topic of choice, and allow him to get to know people a little at a time. Local shows for small planes, antiques, collectible dolls, and classic cars also attract many of the same people again and again. Eventually, you will recognize others and have a chance to interact. Ask if youth versions of the activities are offered, such as youth gardener programs or monthly events at the science museum, where your child can get involved. Even if your child has advanced knowledge in a given subject, many of these programs are designed to value that advanced knowledge rather than squash down the outliers because the central premise is learning about the subject matter rather than being with age peers. That shift of focus from age to interest moves the resentfulness of others for those who are "ahead" of them into appreciation for what they can add. The right kind of encouragement goes a long way and can be a huge benefit of having a mentor, whether formal or informal.

Serendipity

Sometimes, through idle conversation, you will come across someone who can be a resource. You might be at a community event or standing in line at the grocery store, or it could turn out that your friend's cousin knows someone across town who happens to work in a related field and would love to meet your child. Slightly more directed opportunities include intentionally seeking activities your child enjoys and getting to know others through this common interest. For example, a young person who spends a great deal of time volunteering at the soup kitchen or local Head Start program will meet adults who share her passion for helping others. Regular visits to the county animal shelter provide an opportunity to learn about animal care, veterinary work, and local government resources, as well as meet other people interested or working in those areas.

You may be surprised at all the potential resources that you find. Just keep your eyes and ears open.

Overcoming Skepticism

Just because you have identified a potential friend or mentor does not mean that they are necessarily willing to develop a relationship with your child or you. While developing a social life for your child is *your* priority, it is not at the top of everyone else's list. For example, your child might meet another child who is older or younger and is willing to get to know them, but the other child's parents have issues with what they consider to be a large age gap. Or, the other parent may possibly have concerns about your child's behavioral issues, or perhaps you two adults do not hit it off very well. (Sitting for an hour or two with a parent with whom you really do not have much in common, just so that your kids can have a supervised playdate, can be quite difficult.)

With gifted and twice exceptional kids, a handful of specific issues come up again and again, particularly when they are homeschooled or the family is charting its own course in some other way. Your family's choices may make others uncomfortable, or others may be concerned that your family's beliefs may influence their child is a way that they consider negative. Moreover, other parents might feel competitive ("Why is your child reading fluently while mine is just sounding out words?") or they may prefer to steer their child toward friends and activities with which they are comfortable, thinking that

39

your six-year-old's string theory obsession is weird or your 14-year-old's jokes about Schrödinger's cat are disturbing.

When you encounter this sort of resistance or skepticism, you need to determine which opportunities are important enough for to you to invest your time attempting to sway the opinions of others, and which simply are not. Some common problems that pop up over and over again include:

Skepticism from potential mentor or teacher

So many of us have heard "Your child is eight years old and you want to enroll him in my high school science class?" or "I'm sorry, she may be very bright, but I don't think she'll fit in well with the other children." Maybe you encountered a guitar teacher who refused to accommodate your son's needs, despite your son's enthusiasm and early proficiency in playing, informing you that he was there to teach guitar, "not special education."

Other adults may believe that your child will not be able to learn what she wants at the age or in the way that interests her. For example, a seven-year-old decided that she wanted to learn to sew on a proper sewing machine. Her parents had no skill in that area, so they approached various fabric stores where classes were held. They were laughed at outright by several potential teachers who could not conceive of a seven-year-old girl running a computerized sewing machine on her own. After pounding the pavement and following up on referrals, they found a sewing instructor for the little girl: a lady who had recently retired as an engineer in order to work with her own teen daughters on their projects. Over the course of two years, the little girl learned to design her own patterns, used and maintained her computerized sewing machine, and completed a variety of modern and period outfits for herself, her dolls, and for her friends.

Another family we know had a gifted six-year-old son who was very interested in participating in meaningful bible study. His mother approached the pastor of their church to see if he could sit in on some adult sessions. Initially she was rebuffed, due to the pastor's belief that the boy would not understand the material or would derail the conversations of the other participants. His mother handled this by giving the pastor lots of opportunities to observe her son interacting with others in the congregation, along with offering to come with him for a few sessions just to be sure he would adapt to the culture of the class. Eventually, he was able to join the adults and get the intellectual stimulation he was craving. Along the way, her son also found a mentor in his pastor, because of the process she went through to make it possible for him to be in the class. Through the mother's perseverance, she and her son achieved their goal of his engaging more with their religious community.

Skepticism from different-age kids

Imagine you are at the playground with your local homeschool group. A teenager works hard on a drawing, and your younger child wanders over. "What are you drawing? How did you do it? How can I learn how to do that?" A zillion questions fall from her lips, but the teen wants nothing to do with her. The teen may not mind being interrupted, as much as he does not want to be bothered by someone else's annoying younger sibling. "Aw, get out of here, you're going to mess up my project." "But I want to know how to do that, too."

The obvious short-term response is to intervene in some way to reduce the irritation of the teenager, such as pulling child back to you. If you then engage the adolescent yourself, asking questions and showing an interest in a way that will be less intrusive, you create the double benefit of both smoothing the way between the two kids and modeling for your own child how to get a more positive response when approaching someone else.

A longer-term approach might be to see if the teenager is open to a one-on-one visit, so that they may get to know each other. This way, the teen would be better prepared to discuss drawing and less likely to feel intruded upon. Additionally, the older child might be feeling awkward in a group situation because of the age difference, but might actually be very interested in sharing his passion with a younger person, as long as other teens are not watching.

This arrangement can lead to the very challenging situation of your child having a great friend in the teen when it is just the two of them, but the teen not giving your child the time of day back at the park. You can handle this a couple of ways. You could keep the relationship one-on-one and not go to group events with that older friend. If, however, your child wishes to see other friends at those events, it is a great opportunity to have a conversation about "Just like you have friends you want to see at the park, so does your older friend. Let him see them there, and you can look forward to enjoying his company later on when it is just the two of you."

Other parents' skepticism

Sometimes, the parents of the other child object to the relationship. You may have encountered such statements as "Isn't my son a little old for yours?" or "I would never let my daughter read those books/play that video game/go to that activity." Some parents may express concern under the guise of advocating for their own child. One mother we know was told, in an apparently humorous tone, "Well, when our son is acting out, we know it's because he's been around your son." Rudeness aside, this is essentially one parent telling the other, "I don't want my child hanging out with yours." As with any situation, you need to determine if this is a friendship worth pursuing. If so, perhaps a more structured interaction would be satisfactory to all parties. You could possibly enlist mutual friends to try to assist in educating the other parent about your child or simply talk about what a great time their children had with yours, but this assumes you have those resources and that they are willing to help. Unfortunately, it is impossible to change other people's natures or ingrained opinions, so you may get little to no traction on this topic. Choosing to attempt to salvage the relationship will also depend on the ages and maturity of the children in question: a teenager will be more able to make choices about their own friends and relationships than an eight-year-old.

Parents skeptical about you

Sometimes, other parents and adults disapprove or are skeptical of perceived differences in values or behaviors that they attribute to you. They may have a different philosophy of education, parenting style, or religious practice. Some families may be quite convinced that the behavior resulting from neuropsychological diagnoses are actually willful misbehavior by your child, and will consequently peg you as a poor parent. You can attempt to educate them, but you cannot control what someone else chooses to believe. Keep in mind that they may have heard their child's descriptions of kid conversations or interactions of which they do not approve. For example, your child might have been sharing his enthusiasm about a new video game with their child, a game was against their family rules. Similarly, another parent might take umbrage at your child's intense emotional outbursts and wish to keep their child away from yours, whether or not their child wishes to, because they believe that your unwillingness to discipline your child threatens their own child.

Of course, any family should be aware of the topics of conversation between their young children and their children's friends, and any parent of gifted/2e kids should be open to discuss with parents of their child's friends (or potential friends) their child's issues and how they handle them. A sudden break in the relationship does not give the child who brought up the offending topic or is unable to effectively manage their emotional responses the opportunity to learn that different families have different rules, cultures, and values, and that it is a good idea to develop some awareness and sensitivity to those. The child simply feels rejected and like he did something wrong, particularly if it is not something he has developed control over. It can be especially galling to have another parent tell you that your child is an unsuitable playmate, and then be unable to offer an explanation to your child that does not hurt his feelings. Even if you say, "Well, they are just jerks," your child is likely to blame himself or you, because those are the concepts he can master.

Unbalanced Relationships

Sometimes your child will meet someone she really wants to spend time with and it turns out the other person is not quite so interested. Perhaps your child does not have many friends, and while the other child (or adult) enjoys her company, that person also has a lot of other people and activities and far less time for your child. Your child may be disappointed and hurt that the person she thinks of as her "best friend" does not feel the same way, but the lack of reciprocation does not have to be cause for ending the relationship. Not every friendship is equal. It may be better for your child to have someone rather than no one, and the network she gains from the one friend could be a source of other potential friends.

Kids should learn that finding their interests and spending time on them presents valuable opportunities to meet people who share those interests, rather than specifically looking for friends and then having to figure out what to do with them. Focusing on what they enjoy also keeps kids busy so they do not dwell on their loneliness. As a side benefit, the more time they spend developing expertise in their interests, the more attractive they are as a friend to others because they have skills or knowledge to share. A happy, relatively fulfilled person is always more attractive as a friend than a person who mopes around, hiding behind her computer to cover over the pain of loneliness.

Regardless of how unbalanced a relationship may (or may not) be, parents will need to be involved in some way—in the moment for younger kids and as a coach for older kids. Friendship contains so many unwritten rules that may completely befuddle your child, and those rules are not always consistent across relationships. Your child will need and benefit from your involvement.

Geography: Will Travel (Literally or Virtually) for Friends

Sometimes you just cannot find anyone or anything local. Maybe a close friend moves away, or your child makes friends with a classmate in an online course. You may travel great distances to attend summer programs for gifted children and their families, or visit a convention such as Makers Faire, a gem and mineral show, or an historical reenactment where you know there will be others who share your child's interests. The opportunity for your child to spend time among others who share their interests is priceless.

Some families of gifted and twice exceptional kids use travel as a way for their child to spend time with others like them. Others use it to extend their educational opportunities. Still others see travel as a way to keep their child busy learning and meeting people on a short-term basis and avoiding the sense of being left out in their neighborhoods, the difficulties inherent when they can only hold it together for so long, or the people no longer willing to accept their child as is. The interaction with others from different places and backgrounds provides a valuable opportunity for children to see that people are different, as opposed to the sameness of a neighborhood where the child stands out.

Sometimes your child will make a friend who lives far away and that friend, who is not part of his daily interactions, can provide relief from the ongoing drama and difficulties of his local group. It is wonderful when the families can get together for a visit or a camping trip or at a group event and the children fly into each other's arms and start talking together as if they had never been separated. The tears that spring to a parent's eyes from the warmth and fuzziness of these moments are worth whatever it took to get there. Every child should have the opportunity to feel loved by a friend. Some children simply have more difficulty finding that friend.

Chapter Four
Directing: The Parent as Guide

Parenting outlier kids requires more direct involvement than parenting more typical children, and parents may get pushback from others who claim they are "coddling" their child, keeping him artificially dependent, or simply making different parenting choices. The reality is that these children *do* need more intensive parenting at times, and helping them learn the skills to balance their interests with their need for social involvement is one area where parents are vitally important. With gifted and 2e children, there is no substitute for in-the-moment, hands-on direction and support.

Skeptics will tell you that you should leave your child to figure it out herself, and that "directing" is akin to micromanaging and helicopter parenting. However, if your child had been able to figure this all out on her own, you probably would not be reading this book. As a result, we can assume that, despite what others may call it, what you are seeking to do is not to *control* your child's social interactions, but to *scaffold* them, which we will discuss momentarily.

Up until this point, we talked mostly about the philosophy, research, and concepts behind socialization, twice-exceptionality, giftedness, and parenting. We have also made some practical suggestions as to what you can do. Now we will run through some additional concerns that may come up for parents in the course of guiding gifted and 2e kids through social challenges. Assuming the role of "director" may be counter to much of your experience so far, and can sometimes run afoul of the expectations others have for your behavior as a parent. In fact, we have found that holding the idea of being a director—*someone with more context who stays offstage but provides guidance to the players as needed*—relative to your child's social development can facilitate a paradigm shift that will help you feel more comfortable with your involvement in your child's interactions.

Scaffolding

Once you have found a potential friend, companion, or mentor, your job is not over. You may look at those other parents sitting around and chatting at park day and wish you could join them, but realistically, your attention will likely be elsewhere. Parents of kids who are different have the particular challenge of a child who "looks normal" but needs scaffolding. That does not mean you necessarily have to sit with your child and hold his hand in every situation (although you might have to go places with him in some cases, such as a younger child who needs behavioral guidance in a college classroom), but you may need to be within sight and sound of him, able to send private signals or observe enough to help deconstruct whatever might happen at a later time.

Scaffolding is not doing things for your child in order to prevent her from having to do hard work. It is giving your child the support she needs so that she can grow and stretch in other areas without being restricted by her challenges. If your child were missing a leg, instead of letting her stay seated while you got what she wanted for her, you might give her a crutch or prosthetic limb so she could get up and get it herself. Scaffolding can look very different in different contexts, depending on what the child needs. Much like the physical scaffolding used during building construction, it might not always be particularly attractive or graceful, but it is an integral, if temporary, part of helping children reach their desired goals.

For example, many gifted and 2e children have deep passions, even obsessions. They get so wrapped up in their interest that they may forget, or simply not realize, that it does not hold the same interest for others. A parent can be alert to this propensity and help the child learn to tone down obsessions or unusual interests in certain contexts in order to be more approachable or not scare away potential friends or mentors. Rather than implying that the interest is bad in some way, parents can teach children to use their obsession as a way to expand connections by attending meetings with others who share their interest, or to help them to understand how their obsession might "hook into" a different subject for learning or conversing.

Even better is teaching children to use other kids' obsessions as a way to connect, creating a win-win situation. In order to identify others' interests, your child will first need to develop the skill of observation so as to pick up on possible avenues for connection. Parents can scaffold this skill by identifying these interests and pointing out what the kids their child wants to make friends with all seem to be involved in.

With all this scaffolding, you may be concerned that you will never have the opportunity to socialize with the other parents and enjoy your children playing independently. Scaffolding can be temporary and your child will have a time when he can play or participate with others without your feeling the need to breathe down his neck. However, do not assume that one or even a few positive experiences equate to being "all done" with this part of your parental responsibility.

It would be lovely to have a program where you could send your child to learn social skills, and when the program was over you would not have to worry about those issues anymore. You could drop your child off once a week for a few weeks, and at the end of the class he would be suave and debonair and cooperative at all times.

With gifted kids who are socially awkward, recommendations are frequently made to "social skills groups," either within a school setting or at a speech therapy practice. For children who need the benefit of learning a rubric to help them navigate social interactions, this can be a useful addition to their learning—sometimes a child needs to be taught didactically what others pick up intuitively. But for the child who needs support beyond the learning of the rubric, or for those who need to move on after learning these basics, the traditional social skills group is insufficient. Within the group setting, much of the learning covers common, general behaviors such as manners, listening before talking, conversation starters, and so on. The gifted or twice exceptional child needs more nuance and specificity to cover all of the "what ifs?" that come up in each unique interaction. A full toolbox is useless if you do not know when to use each tool. And using a tool with only partial skill still can add difficulty to social interactions.

Moreover, a significant difference lies between what kind of behavior a child can expect from others in a group who are all working on the same skills, especially under the watchful eye of a trained professional, and what behavior that child might encounter in the wild. Indeed, one of the frequent pieces of feedback we hear from children who have completed groups like this is bewilderment that "even though I did everything right, just like I learned in group, the other kid didn't behave the way I expected." Apparently, the other child did not participate in the group and get the memo.

This is a wonderful, but hard, training ground for the lesson that you can control your own behavior and choices, but not those of other people. This is also an indication that your child is going to need more nuanced tools and experiences, since her group has not prepared her for this. It can be useful to have a separate "tool kit" for "what do I do when I don't know what to do," a buffet of choices that might include hanging back and watching for a bit, checking in with a known friend (perhaps another child or an adult), explaining to others what is going on inside their own head, or asking for very specific directions on how to join the group. Be prepared to provide empathy and normalize the experience of frustration when others do not behave the way your child thinks they should. Sharing personal examples of this situation with your child will help her see that this is a universal struggle, not a personal failing.

Children who are trying to integrate into social situations with other children find it particularly challenging because the range of behaviors in children, particularly in a low supervision setting, is much more varied and unpredictable than those of adults. This is one reason why socially struggling children are frequently described as "prefers the company of adults" on school reports: the adults are simply more predictable and have more experience with a range of behaviors, which means they are less likely to be startled. Additional opportunities for learning come out of this kind of interaction: first, your child can see that other children are still learning their own social skills, and second, your child may realize how she and her actions can appear to others.

While your child needs to understand that her poorly thought out statements may hurt others, it is equally important that she not always hear it from Mom and Dad. Important tips such as "If you don't wash regularly, people won't want to be around you" or "I know you think those jokes are funny, but after two or three repetitions, it's just annoying" might best come from another adult with whom your child has a trusting relationship. Negative social interactions with other children can also be analyzed later, when you can discuss with your child the unspoken meaning behind a particular behavior.

Having a child whose needs are atypical can be a huge challenge. You cannot always predict what will work and what will not. As a result, you make your best guess and then hope for a positive outcome. When it is clearly not working out, you have to carefully choose your next step. On the one hand, you do not want to put your child in a position where she is almost certain to melt down. On the other hand, you are trying to model responsibility, which means following through on your commitments. In your own head, you may be arguing with yourself over whether you are making excuses or explanations. You also may worry about the impact on others, even though it is not really their problem.

We suggest managing this by taking the following steps:

- Slightly compress or downsize the commitment. For example, can you end a week earlier?

- Plan ahead with your child what you will do if it gets too hard and how each of you will manage your stress.

- Provide support and scaffolding so that it is as positive an experience as possible when he is there. For example, do not send him to do hard tasks all alone, but realize you may be faced with potential criticism from others who say you are undermining his independence. Ignore it. You know what your child needs.

- When it is over, discuss it and share your perspectives. Was it as bad as you or he thought it would be? What parts went well? What can you do better next time?

Listening

Parents may unwittingly mistake their own upbringing or social paradigm with the actual needs of their children. As parents, we have an opportunity to learn from our children, if only we *listen* to them. For example, one mother we know was very excited that her daughter was being included among the most popular girls in their social group, because the mother had been left out when she was a child. It turned out, though, that the girl was not excited about popularity and really was not enjoying their company. She told her mother that, in the future, she would actually prefer fewer playdates with those girls and more with the few children with whom she felt particularly close. The mother had been projecting her own feelings without considering what made her daughter happy, but by listening, she learned something about herself. In fact, the mother took this as "permission" to reconsider her own life, and discovered that she felt quite similarly. Her childhood had been so full of pressure to participate in the "in" social activities that it had become an important part of her personal value system, one that never had sat right with her.

In addition to listening to your child's words, listen *through* their words to understand what she is trying to communicate. Time, context, and emotions all play a role in meaning, as do apraxia and other language processing difficulties. A child may say, "I hate Regina and I never want to see her again," when what she actually means is,

"Regina's house is loud and echo-y and her bigger siblings tease us and nobody cares." The former is a statement of emotion, while the latter is a nuanced problem statement that might actually be solved together.

One of the factors at play here is a tendency for gifted or 2e children to look at a problem (for example, visits at Regina's house are stressful), and jump to a single conclusion to solve the problem (never see Regina again). Gifted and 2e kids do this for a variety of reasons, the most common of which is that they have developed a habit of thought where they believe that the first idea that comes to them must be correct. Frequently, especially in an academic context, this works well enough (such as solving a math problem without showing the work), but it can leave them without opportunities to practice being flexible and creative in their overall problem solving. Additionally, gifted kids may struggle to articulate the root problem of a given scenario due to the asynchrony between their lived experience and their emotional vocabulary. Rather than spell out the specific problem she is experiencing (due to embarrassment, lack of confidence, inability to identify it for themselves), the child approaches her parent with a single, not particularly nuanced solution. If the parent enters the scene at this point, with no background, the conversation ends up being about *whether* to be friends with Regina rather than *how* to be friends with Regina. Of course, a child is perfectly entitled not to like Regina anymore, but it would be a shame to miss out on all the potential positives that would arise if the specific problems were solved, and seeing Regina once more became pleasant. When the child has committed to the first solution that comes to mind, it leads to a lot of confusion about what the problem actually is. The parent sees only that the child seemed to enjoy her friend before, and now she claims to hate her. The parent is essentially working blind. When, however, the parent and child together can retrace the steps back to the specific problem, they can consider a variety of options and choose the one that fits best.

Ultimately, some gifted and 2e kids need translation help. You may need to use your deeper understanding of your child to draw out more specific information about what he is trying to communicate. He does not need others to literally read his mind, but he knows what he wants to say and may have trouble putting the right words together to articulate the message he wants to convey. This is not to say that you should never take your child's statements at face value, but instead that a certain amount of intuition, understanding, and unraveling may be required for more sensitive subjects and situations. Sometimes, the only way that you can be certain that you understand what your child needs is by listening and repeating back to him, and allowing him to confirm or deny. To not do so is to ignore the child's thoughts and feelings and leave him feeling disrespected, unimportant, and vulnerable to manipulation or misunderstanding (deliberate or otherwise) by others who have conflicting agendas.

Negotiating

In addition to real-time guidance for your child, you may also find yourself having to approach parents, teachers, mentors, and other adults to discuss your child's relationship with them or with their child. Though these attempts to communicate or advocate for your child can be extremely helpful with resolving uncertain situations, they can also lead to discomfort or even the termination of that particular relationship. When trying to enlist other parents in developing your child's friendship, some of them may read your words and actions as criticism of their parenting choices or even of their child. A mentor or instructor might feel defensive about her teaching techniques, which have been successful with many others in the past, and not welcome your insights into how your child thinks.

In some situations, you will need to negotiate entrance to an activity before the other adults have even met your child. A game shop may have a weekly Dungeons and Dragons game and the Dungeon Master may feel that the presence of your tween would inhibit the somewhat more mature joking around by other participants. Similarly, organizers of a Magic: The Gathering tournament may be concerned that your child will hold up the game or be unable to participate appropriately. Applications to volunteer may also garner similar responses; in addition to legal liability, the staff may feel that having a child involved with their organization would be a net loss of supervisory time rather than a gain in work output.

In any of these situation, you can offer the perennial favorite, "But I'll come along and sit in/participate, too!" Also, you can offer the people concerned a chance to get to know your child prior to the activity. Perhaps they would be open to a trial period wherein the child either first comes along to observe or gets involved for a short time to determine if it is a positive experience for everyone involved. Keep your eye on your goal. Are you trying to appease other parents' concerns about your child's behavior in order to continue attending a park day group? Then they need to understand enough about your child to feel comfortable having her continue in the group. Asking others what they need in order to feel comfortable beginning or continuing any given situation may be a particularly useful starting point or a litmus test. If they come up with specific issues, you have a way forward. If they say there is nothing you can do, then you need to walk away and find a more welcoming environment.

Put yourself in the shoes of the other person. After all, while our children deserve opportunities to experience the world, the world does have the right not to be unduly imposed upon. It would be nice if everyone understood and accommodated, but the fact is that often they do not. Our children are outliers and they are deserving, but they are not entitled. Sometimes we want so badly to make a situation work that we push and push, but that is not a good idea. Bulldozing someone into agreement often sets everyone up for bad feelings and likely failure. While we can visualize how great it would be for our child if the situation worked out, we need to accept the reality that sometimes it just will not. "Successful" forcing will not give us what we hope for, and sometimes we need to choose between the bulldozed version or no involvement at all.

Adult-to-adult conversations can smooth the way for your child; you won't know unless you try. You do, however, have to be willing to take a hit and keep coming back. Eventually, you may successfully obtain a trial run for your child, but negotiations may continue. As an activity progresses over time, you may need to advocate repeatedly on behalf of your child. Keep in mind that many adults appreciate constructive input regarding difficult situations, particularly when they want to make the situation work. Complimenting them on ways they have been successful is a good place to start; no one likes to hear criticism, intended or otherwise.

Explaining your child's needs and behaviors as neurological can be quite helpful in some cases. For example, do not be afraid to use labels even if they do not fully describe your child. For example, if your child has severe sensory reactions to something, it might be easiest for your listener to hear, "If you treat him like you would treat many children on the autism spectrum, those accommodations have a good chance of being effective." This gives the other adult a mental "hook" to work with. They have likely heard of "autism spectrum" before, so they do not need to spend time wrapping their minds around it. Also, try empathic hooks, such as, "You know how you might walk into a Walmart and suddenly feel like your head is going to explode due to the lights and echoes? That's how my child feels in certain environments. That auditory and visual chaos actually hurts her." What you are doing is both explaining your child's needs as well as validating your child's feelings *to the adult*, which can be handy when adults do not view children's individual needs as deserving of the same respect they would offer to an adult peer.

Another critical part of negotiation is understanding another person's perspective. You cannot adequately advocate for your own child if you do not understand your child's behavior yourself. Therefore, you must ask questions of your child before taking action. For example, one typical situation involves another adult informing you that your child just walked up and hit another person "for no good reason." Of course, no one should intentionally hit anyone other than in self defense—and therein lies the problem. Rather than simply assume that your child is a bad kid who needs correction, take a moment to consider what precipitated the event. Perhaps your child is sensory defensive and other children were crowding him (even in a friendly manner), or maybe he felt emotionally provoked beyond his breaking point (and human beings do have breaking points). Given these, or other similar situations, he may have simply lost his still-developing self-control, been unable to retrieve an appropriate tool from his emotional tool box, and swung at the other child in what he perceived to be self defense. Children deserve the benefit of the doubt even more so than adults because they are still learning and their brains are still developing. That is not to say that we should dismiss the entire situation as meaningless, but rather that we should look at the behaviors as red flags and respond proactively and constructively. Holding a child to adult behavioral standards is unreasonable, and often an adult advocate needs to remind those around the child of this in the heat of the moment.

A final factor in negotiation may include addressing whatever stereotypes others use to label you or your child. Others may see your child as a stuck up brat or a problem child; they may see you as a pushy parent who is urging your child along for your own vanity. You will have to patiently move forward with *your* situation and hope the rest of the world eventually catches on. You may unwittingly end up as a poster child for giftedness, or homeschooling, or twice exceptionality. It is uncomfortable to feel judged in any case; it is more so when you are seen as representative of such a large and diverse population. Stay focused on your goals and your child's needs.

Teaching Cultural Literacy

Part of the process of putting on a play includes costume design and props. Likewise, personal appearance and the ability to fit in have always been crucial factors in the formation of human social bonds. "Fitting in" may not be the be-all and end-all of your efforts, but your child needs to be able to identify key elements and make an informed decision as to how she wishes to appear. Our children need to understand *how* a person might fit in and how others might view them, then make choices. Younger children may be more malleable on this point, while teenagers may have their own ideas or groups they wish to represent. Some children may find it "silly" to learn that others will judge them by their appearance, but they also need to understand the reality of the situation. If they want to fit in with a particular group, they may not even get in the door if they look too different. This applies not just to fashion statements but to basic hygiene. A teenager who is too busy reading or programming to remember to brush her hair and use deodorant on a regular basis may end up with a rat's nest on her head and no one wanting to come near her. The child who hangs on to a dearly loved but poorly fitting pair of jeans, or a t-shirt with childhood characters on it may need to know that he is making a statement that he does not consciously intend to make.

If you are not sure how to approach this issue, perhaps you can take your child to places where there are a variety of people, such as the mall, the park, or a sidewalk café, and have a running dialogue about what you and your child each see. You can also watch favorite movies or television shows, although those may be less timely or even less appropriate, depending on the topic and genre. People-watching, whether in-person or on the screen, is a good way to discuss social behaviors: "That person is leaning over a book and scowling; what do you think she is thinking? How do you think she would react if someone approached her?" "Do you see how those teens are walking? Some are grouped together while others are hanging around the fringes." "When you see those boys playing with Nerf guns at the playground, observe how they interact. Who seems to be the leader? Are there others he listens to? When another child wants to join in, what happens? How welcoming are they to new people?" Because each group of people will react and respond in different ways, you may need to walk your child through this process repeatedly, making a point of noting the local cultural and behavioral mores and expectations.

In addition to clothing, there are topics that may be good conversation starters in most settings. Star Wars, Doctor Who, Pokémon, My Little Pony, popular books, movies, and TV shows—all of these can be turned into fodder for conversation when a child wants to have social interactions. Encouraging your child to know something about the subject will keep him from feeling completely bewildered around his age peers. Balancing individual needs (such as obsessions or sensitivities) with a passing familiarity with what everyone else is talking about or playing provides our children with something to bond over and learn social skills from.

Constructing a workaround is possible for situations where, for example, parents do not think the full exposure to a film is appropriate for their child, but they want their child to have the background knowledge anyway. In the case of a movie like Star Wars, parents can get a bunch of figurines and play out the stories with a young child who may be too sensitive to watch the movies, or go to the library and pick up a few of the "kid-friendly," watered-down versions of the story in question. Look into visual encyclopedias and YouTube clips that discuss aspects of a story or character without getting into anything too violent or graphic. With a little creative thinking, you can find ways to appropriately share common cultural experiences with your child so that she can connect with the kids in her playgroup who are all obsessed with that particular iconic geekiness. Once your child has seen the characters and heard some of the background stories, she is fully equipped to join in pretend games based on those themes without actually having seen the movies. Specifically, she will know what a light saber is and why the other kids are saying "interesting, that is."

Cultural literacy is *not* the same as bowing to trends that conflict with your personal values or preferences. We are not suggesting that if you don't "get in line," you will be disliked or ostracized, although that may well be the case in some situations. Unfortunately, kids who are inclined to tease and bully will always find or create a reason. The critical point is that you have to figure out your own balance and boundaries and then help your child find his. With some creative thinking, you can give him the basic information and tools to participate in an age-peer based conversation without compromising your values.

Dealing with Authorities

Another aspect of guiding your child through the social world includes preparing her to play different roles in different situations. Children often act differently with adults than with young people. When they are called upon to shift from one to another, those shifts may not be as smooth as we would like. One of the situations where addressing the transition to a different role is vital is in scenarios involving safety and dealing with authorities.

Accepting your child and all of his quirks and uniqueness is wonderful. Particularly when they are young, children need to know that who they are is OK and that they are worthy of love and understanding. As they get older, however, some of those traits can create social rifts, and they can also cause trouble with employers, public safety officers, and others in positions of authority. The wise-cracking gifted teenager who mouths off to a store security guard could find himself being arrested by actual cops and charged with disorderly conduct, particularly if there are onlookers. An unwillingness to cooperate or an inability to follow directions quickly (without time to process the order, and without being able to ask what the officer means) could result in injuries and imprisonment for resisting arrest. A child reacting with sensory defensiveness could be perceived as assaulting an officer. Auditory processing disorder could lead to all kinds of miscommunication, and a well-intended compliment about the officer's weaponry could have unfortunate results.

While we really hate having to discuss this at all—it is scary, and we all know it—we also recognize that if we do not plan ahead, our children could develop behaviors that are potentially dangerous. What seems cute in a young child may be less so as she gets older and bigger, and what was acceptable for a child may be viewed differently in someone who appears to be a young adult. While parents cannot be responsible for the unreasonable or ambiguous demands of others, we can be proactive in teaching our children how to respond in order to minimize escalation. We can talk with our children about problems that may arise due to their different processing or perceptions, and give them specific tools to work with. Role playing can also be tremendously helpful, with the caveat that you may wish to find someone who is not their parent to take on some of the roles. Children frequently assume their parents understand what is going on inside their heads, and practicing only with parents can lead to the assumption that *all* adults know what is going on inside their heads, which is another risk factor for misunderstandings. We say all this not to scare you, but to give you the tools to prepare your kids for the world beyond you.

Chapter Five

Showtime: Applying What You Know

How do parents know they are doing the right thing? That is the $64,000 question. We want to know, as people with our own gifted and perfectionistic tendencies, what behavior on our part results in the "correct" behavior at the end of the day. We may have our own insecurities about parenting or we simply fear failing our child. We may hope that when our children engage in a group activity that they will get along with the others, learn self-control and patience, and generally be a credit to their upbringing, while at the same time fearing it will work out very differently.

Our kids are rarely ever going to fit the generic mold. At some point, we will have to get out there and try different things, collect data, and make choices. We need to encourage our kids to do the same in order to find friends and alleviate loneliness. While it would be great if a friendly child would walk up to your child, introduce herself, and be your child's immediate best friend, that is not usually what happens. As Piglet in Winnie the Pooh once said, "You can't stay in your corner of the Forest waiting for others to come to you. You have to go to them sometimes." So be brave. You can do this!

Stage Fright: Yours and Theirs

Every parent of a gifted or twice-exceptional child fears for and worries about their child. Keep in mind that it is pretty rare to find a kid without any social anxieties. You and your child are not alone.

Here are some common questions and worries:

What should I do when my child resists receiving help or refuses to try something because she has a disability or challenge that makes it hard?

This question covers two sides of the same coin: the child who insists she can do it alone and the child who refuses to try anything at all. Even though on the face of it these two situations appear diametrically opposed, the factors at play are similar. Both can come out of a child's self-story about what a particular situation will or should be like, before she has actually experienced it. One story is of high capability and the other of low, but both can be inaccurate assessments on the part of the child. The real problem is that the child becomes too attached to a particular expectation of herself and the experience.

This calls for help from a parent to relax or open views of what to expect, which can be done in a number of ways. In the case of a child who is predicting disaster and refusing to participate, playing the "What's the worst that could happen?" game can be effective. Participants take turns imagining horrible outcomes, frequently devolving into the silly or absurd. The process can loosen up a child's worries and help bring some perspective and proportion to her fears, allowing a parent to do reality-based problem-solving and planning.

In the case of the child who is over-confident, sometimes it behooves parents to play the "What's the worst that could happen?" game with their own worries. Once parents have adjusted their own level of worry, they will find it easier to negotiate with their children about providing assistance on an as-needed basis.

We parents are often torn between wanting to see our children become as independent as possible and not setting them up for failure, particularly when we know that one failure may send them running so far away that it will be a long time before they are willing to try again. Just because a child is young does not mean he will be unable to handle a situation, nor does a child being older mean that he will. It depends on a variety of factors, the most critical of which is the gap between the needed skill level for a given activity and the child's actual ability. Even though we usually have a pretty good idea of what our children can handle and how they will react, this can be difficult to gauge because our kids are constantly surprising us. Think about the individual situation and the people involved. For example, would another adult provide support so you can back off, or will you be needed for more direct scaffolding? Does your child prefer to learn things the hard way, or does he seem open to a little shared wisdom? What is the level of risk if he fails: is it likely to have a big or long-term effect, or is he likely to learn from it and move on? What about the amount of effort that will be required from you in pulling it off, as well as in cleaning up the mess afterward if it does not work out? We love to see our children march off to face their challenges, but it can be heartbreaking (as well as time-consuming and costly) to put them back together afterward, if needed.

What should I do when my child is pursuing a friendship out of loneliness rather than a good fit?

As we have discussed previously, humans share a basic need for friendship and companionship. It is worth noting that these are not necessarily the same thing. A companion is simply someone to spend time with, although a companion may eventually become a true friend. However, companions are somewhat easier to secure and a lonely child will hang out with almost anyone when she feels sufficiently pressured or desperate. Unfortunately, the process of getting to know her companion better can also lead them to develop a friendship that she might be better off filtering out. Going on the "beggars can't be choosers" principle, gifted and 2e kids may find themselves making poor choices or using poor judgment.

One complicating factor is the changeable nature of children's friendships over time, due to normal developmental changes and external factors like families moving to new communities. Children can find themselves holding on to old friendships that have passed their expiration date rather than looking ahead to make new, appropriate ones, or they may try to model their new friendships on the old ones simply because they know how it is "supposed" to look.

Explaining cycles of friendship to children is no easy task, especially with children who have rigid thinking or anxieties about change. Some may also have trouble understanding why their old friends are not really available any longer, whether due to personal issues, incompatible scheduling, or simply a lack of interest. Parents do not want to think that someone might actually lose interest in their child, much less have to explain that to their child, but that is reality. It happens to children and adults and it feels personal because it is personal. That said, both adults and children need to learn to accept that friendships evolve and sometimes it is best to move on.

What should I do when my child is rejected for reasons which seem particularly arbitrary to them?

Parents need to help their child be as prepared as possible to deal with the rejection of both children and other adults. Unfortunately, sometimes rejection has little or nothing to do with your child and everything to do with seemingly arbitrary characteristics or beliefs. For example, perhaps you have moved to a new community and your daughter is excited about joining the local homeschool group, but they will not allow you to participate because you ascribe to a different religious faith. Perhaps the six-year-olds on the playground will not let your four-year-old join in because he is "too young" and "can't keep up," despite knowing nothing else about him. Perhaps your child has been excluded from an activity because she has language processing difficulties and one of the supervising adults has concerns that she might not be able to communicate with the other children adequately. Of course you could accommodate her disability, but when the rejection comes from the top down, it may pervade the group.

Arbitrary rejection is hard for an adult to swallow, never mind an intelligent, sensitive child. Explaining hard truths about the world to a child you long to protect requires painful conversations, but you will need to have them. Leaving children hanging without a reasonable explanation or understanding can be more damaging than avoiding the topic and hoping it goes away. (It won't. Don't underestimate your child's observations and perceptions.) Happily, many books for kids address these issues, from picture books for young children to teen/young adult novels that explore the topics in depth. Finding other children who have faced similar difficulties or seeking out resources via online communities can also be healing. (See *Resources*.)

In some cases, you may find that you can prepare your child for the possibility of rejection. If you are right and that happens, you may have given them some insulation against the hurt. While you do not want your children to assume they will be rejected, providing self-preservation skills for their emotional toolbox is a good thing to do. When a child is rejected, if she handles it well it can help her situation or make it less bad; but if she handles it poorly in the moment, it can lead to further rejection as well as bullying or loss of access to that environment (such as getting tossed from a classroom or activity). Once again, parents must walk that line in deciding what is too much, too little, or just right for their child.

What should I do when I can see that my child is being rejected or excluded, but he is not yet aware of it?

This is one of the toughest questions to answer for any parent, especially if the rejection is within the context of an activity or interest that is highly valued by your child. It can be helpful to observe the culture of the group, and try to figure out if this exclusionary behavior is the norm, or is an aberration. Sometimes a conversation with an adult in charge can give you that information. You can get a sense of what the group norm is based on the adult's response, and decide whether you wish to keep your child in that group or not. Usually, if the other adults are not sensitive to exclusion or bullying, you will not be able to change the system quickly enough to protect your child.

Which brings us to another, related question: *How do I approach my child when I decide to remove him from an activity that he wishes to continue?* Again, this is an incredibly difficult situation to manage. Probably the best you can make of it is to turn it into an opportunity to teach better observation skills to your child. Sending him the message that you are not going to tolerate his being treated poorly, even when he fails to notice, is also important. In some cases, you may want to feign an urgent text message and call him away in the moment. In other situations, you might wait until the immediate activity is over, keeping in mind that once he does understand what was happening, he is likely to feel hurt and humiliated. Minimizing that hurt by cutting short the interaction may be a better approach.

How do I know if I am encouraging dependency in my child by the actions I take?

At times you might find yourself wondering if (or being accused of by others that) your level of scaffolding is actually getting in the way of your child's growth. Referring back to the description of your role as director, you may find it helpful to evaluate the "safe, structured, and supportive" aspects of parenting. Are you *preventing* your child from having experiences that are challenging? Or, are you *enabling* more of those growth opportunities as a result of your choices? You can consider your child's personal developmental trajectory over time and observe patterns of social growth. Talk with your child and see what she thinks. It may not be your job to gain your child's approval, but it certainly would be beneficial to get feedback from the child you are parenting, whether you agree with her or not. Just keep in mind the long term goal of raising your unique child to become an independent adult and the rest of the pieces will (to some extent) fall into place.

Making Your Entrance

Once you and your child have summoned the courage to get out there and give it a go, create a mental framework for how you are going to approach any given situation. Two such approaches that can be especially useful are method acting and "fake it 'til you make it."

Method acting (and how homeschooling can help)

In line with the goal of raising your children to an independent and successful adulthood, you need to provide them the opportunity to practice a variety of social interactions in a safe space, possibly with you or another caring adult there for support. The theater world calls this method acting, where the actor conjures up memories of real-life experiences and uses them to inform his performance. In a sense, the performer is no longer "acting," but rather showing and sharing his true experiences to the audience.

What kids learn from being out in the world and interacting with a variety of other people in many situations is far better practice for their adults lives, when they are unlikely to spend large periods of time sitting quietly in a room with 30 other same-age, demographically similar adults. Often, the easiest way to have the flexibility to seek out opportunities is to homeschool. Homeschooling, defined in this case as a range of alternative educational options outside of the full-time traditional classroom, can be seen as a kind of method acting. Like method acting, homeschooling gives children the opportunity to practice engaging with a similar range of people and activities as they might encounter in adult life. They are essentially rehearsing for adult life, while the stakes are much lower. Many families who turn to homeschooling for academic or other reasons find that these real life experiences and endless opportunities for practicing new and emerging social skills are among the most significant benefits of homeschooling.

The social flexibility of homeschooling allows the gifted or 2e child to maximize interactions when she can and withdraw when she is overwhelmed. Adults have the opportunity to build lives that allow for a strategic retreat when necessary, whereas kids in traditional school rarely do. Homeschooling mimics the adult reality, providing families the choice to reschedule classes and activities until the child is in a less fragile state. Not only will the child benefit more from academics when she is not so emotionally labile, but she is less likely to display the poor social skills that can lead to bullying or ostracism. From a social-emotional standpoint, homeschooling parents can be more available to help their child navigate difficult situations as they occur. A highly sensitive child need not learn socialization by the "sink or swim" method on the playground.

Fake it 'til you make it

Trying out new social situations and pushing the edge of the envelope provoke quite a bit of anxiety—for kids and parents. Start small. Remember to breathe. Decide to behave as if you were already comfortable. This "fake it 'til you make it" approach, especially when presented as a role the child can play, can greatly lower the apprehension of trying new tools and skills. This approach differs from the method acting idea in that parents and children can emotionally detach from events as they occur. Because the child feels as though he is merely pretending, at least part of the time, incorporating feedback is easier. Any criticism the child receives is of the role he was playing, and not of him personally. Moreover, once the child has "faked it" a number of times, he may realize that "Hey, maybe I can do this thing after all."

"Fake it 'til you make it" can also be reassuring to parents concerned about how their children will perform. Viewing events as "practice sessions" lowers your anxiety, which will almost certainly reflect in your child's behavior. Calmly reacting to situations increases the likelihood your child will too, and minimize any harm done by those who are not supportive.

Chapter Six
Reviews: Raspberries and Applause

Some people will always feel entitled to judge how others parent and educate their children. When you have a relationship with these people that matters to you, their judgment can be hard to handle. Remember, you know your child best. You are the one your child runs to with her joys and sorrows, and you see her at times when those judging never will. You see behind the facade that your child may put on for the public's benefit. You get to choose whether or not to address people's concerns, but we can address some of the biggest criticisms thrown at families of gifted and twice-exceptional children, particularly those who take advantage of homeschooling and other educational alternatives.

People are often wary of things they are not familiar with. The general public misclassifies giftedness as achievement-based, elitist, or simply irrelevant, leaving most people to focus on visible differences, such as behaviors, and judge them without sufficient data. Twice exceptionality has been largely unknown or disavowed. Homeschooling (or any non-traditional educational setting) comes under scrutiny by those who hold antiquated notions of what it might entail, despite the readily accessible information demonstrating differently.

The Gifted and 2e Socialization Question

Parents encounter many questions triggered by "outside the box" behaviors by their gifted or 2e children. A bystander may comment about how a parent let her child "get away with things" or how poorly behaved that child appears when he is experiencing sensory overwhelm. A well-meaning teacher or coach might express concern over the classic "junior prefers to spend time with adults instead of his age peers," with the subtext of "And what exactly do you plan to do about that?" Regardless of whether or not they are entitled to demand answers from you about your parenting, this can end up being a very challenging place to find yourself.

Sometimes you may feel that the questioner has a right to an answer from you, such as when she is a family member or a close friend who has been a part of your life and who truly cares about you and your child. Sometimes you may feel, for whatever reason, that although she is not entitled to an answer, it is in your child's best interest to respond in some reasonably polite way. We suggest beginning with a disarming statement that agrees with at least some part of the comment. An example might be, "Yes, Junior does that sometimes, and yes, it is different from what these other kids are doing." Next, find a way to educate that other person, either sharing information about your child in particular, such as "And we are so pleased to see that Junior is doing so well," or about gifted and 2e kids in general, such as "Did you know that in some kids, this is just a way of calming down from overstimulation? I have found this is an indicator that Junior needs a break." (See the free brochures available at http://giftedhomeschoolers.org/about-us/gifted-children-brochures/.)

Yes, this gets old after the hundredth time, but affirming a positive view of your child holds significant power. If you detect an edge of hostility or disapproval, respond as though the intent was good, whether or not you believe that. Acting as if you assume the best will prevent you from defending yourself or your child, whereas taking a defensive stance usually just degrades the interaction, validating the original negative interpretation. Often, judgmental people are really questioning whether you are raising your child in a way that makes *them* comfortable. Critics may be displeased with your child's seemingly inappropriate behavior and judge your parenting for it, while being completely unaware of any situational context or even of how much of an improvement the behavior is compared to months or years past.

Educational professionals have largely co-opted the public dialogue of giftedness as one of achievement and elitism. Thus, we should not be surprised when the random questioner is completely unaware of the neurological and psychological aspects of giftedness and Dabrowski's Overexcitabilities. Lay people rarely recognize the validity of twice-exceptionality and understand how much of a challenge it places on the child and the entire family. As a result, they are understandably skeptical of how we, as parents, are doing our jobs because how we parent may not look anything like how they understand a "good parent" to look. It then becomes our job to make the effort to educate when and how we can, within the constraints of the demands already placed on us by meeting the special needs of our children. We may not be able to work miracles, but we can plant seeds.

The Homeschool Socialization Question

Parents considering homeschooling often face the socialization question. It goes like this:

> Neighbor: I hear you are homeschooling your children this year?
>
> Mom: Oh, yes, we're a little nervous but very excited.
>
> Neighbor: Hmmm, I'm sure you are. But tell me, what are you going to do about socialization?

Most homeschoolers respond with a list of the many classes, activities, and events they plan to participate in, in order to assure their neighbor that their child will not be duct-taped to the kitchen table all day doing workbooks in the dark. In fact, homeschoolers have numerous opportunities to get out and be sociable with other homeschoolers or with mixed groups of children and adults. Many homeschooled kids are perfectly normal (whatever that means) in appearance or behavior, and their parents are *still* asked this question.

So you can probably imagine (if you have not already experienced it) how this works with kids who are a bit quirky. People often assume that the kids are quirky *because* they are homeschooled. In fact, often the kids are homeschooled because they are already a little different and do not fit in well with a traditional school environment. Being placed in school will not make them less quirky; rather, it will probably make their quirks more obvious and problematic.

Keep in mind that people prefer familiarity. When presented with something they have a negative preconception about, however inaccurate it might be, or something they simply do not know anything about, people understandably address it first with fear or concern. Given time, we hope people will open themselves to this new idea. The trick is to address the fear or discomfort without feeling judged or getting defensive and without jumping all over a well-meaning individual. Though our job is not to make others comfortable with the choices we make on behalf of our children, we should recognize that part of our modeling of socialization is demonstrating for our children how to get along with others on a long-term basis.

The "Get with the Program" Question

When your child is quirky or taking a different path, sometimes the boundaries and guidance you provide may look to others as if you are excusing your child from doing what society thinks all children should be compelled to do. Whether it is allowing more freedom in choosing her own study materials, deciding to skip grades, or preferring to wear her hair in a less mainstream style, you will come across someone who feels the need to express a negative opinion. Do not forget that questioning authority, accommodating sensory issues, and having (and expressing) their own opinions are all typical characteristics of gifted and 2e children. As long as your parenting style acknowledges and works with those needs, you are doing fine.

One aspect of "getting with the program" has to do with behavior in the here and now. Many adults believe in the value of compliance and normalcy, wherein the child should do what he should do simply because "that is how children should behave." For example, an adult may expect children to sit quietly and eat their meal—in McDonald's, even—because those are the manners the adult was taught. Or the receptionist at the doctor's office might be appalled at a child who calls their parents by their first names rather than "mother" and "father." These folks are often made uncomfortable by unexpected behaviors and feel the need to urge parents to discipline their children to make the kids seem more "normal" to outsiders.

Likewise, some adults will express disdain for accommodations used by asynchronous or twice-exceptional kids to assist with their academic and social functioning, seeing those accommodations as crutches which prevent the child from learning a needed skill. Many people do not understand neurological differences and view these diagnoses simply as excuses to avoid hard work. In this case, "getting with the program" means eliminating accommodations and buckling down to do whatever is expected of their age peers, regardless of need or ability. They reason that "these accommodations don't exist in the 'real world' so it's high time your child learned to cope without them." They are wrong. Many accommodations are available for disabled adults, as are a wide array of life choices that children do not generally have available to them. Moreover, many of these difficulties are developmental delays which will eventually become easier for children to manage; they just are not there yet.

Still another aspect of "getting with the program" is the belief that children need to do things a certain way in order to become a functional, employable, socially acceptable adult. For example, many skeptics will question whether a child who takes a non-traditional path can possibly get into college, and if he does, whether he won't be miserable or in an inappropriate setting due to his age and life experience. People may also ask if the child will learn what she needs to know to be a good employee if she is constantly questioning rules or behaving in ways that the questioner deems unacceptable. In fact, many adults have fixed paradigms about how the world works and often have trouble keeping up as things change. As it happens, many colleges and employers actively open up alternative pathways to entry, because inquisitiveness, initiative, and creative thinking are precisely what is needed for the economy in which these kids will participate. That is not always an easy sell for adults who have spent their formative years and the bulk of their professional lives in a markedly different setting.

Regardless of the reason for this kind of criticism, understand it as the critic's issue and not yours or your child's. Certainly, if your child is doing something that actively disturbs others or causes harm, you will want to take action. If the critic merely does not understand that you have made an informed choice about your parenting and it is not a matter of your not knowing any better, then take it with a grain of salt and either let it slide or, when appropriate, share your reasoning. They may learn something!

Epilogue
Take a Bow

Choosing an approach that is not what others expect or approve of is rarely easy. Everyone has an opinion—justified or not—which they are more than happy to share. Bucking the system may make others uncomfortable; however, what works for "everyone else" is irrelevant to *your* family because the child you are raising is an individual, he is not *everyone else*. One of the most important parts of raising a child is preparing him for his own adulthood. That means remembering who he is and what makes him unique, and responding to that rather than defaulting to a societal template of "How to be an Adult." Success comes in many flavors, and the lives of adults 10 or 20 years in the future may include options we cannot yet imagine. Our job is to help our kids become comfortable with who they are, know what they need, and learn how to get it—a broader view of success, and one that is far more adaptable to unknown futures.

We hope you feel more comfortable doing what *you* think is best in supporting your gifted or twice exceptional child. You can successfully put together a suite of people and activities that allows your child to not just "get along" but to thrive, and be the best self they can. You will almost certainly encounter bumps in the road, but ultimately, if you can remain focused on the goal of social and emotional well-being, it will come out fine. In fact, it will probably come out even better than you could ever have imagined. Trust your instincts, trust your child, and embrace writing your own script—yours will be far better than one blandly written for mass distribution.

You either write your own script, or you become an actor in someone else's script. [11]

~John Taylor Gatto

Resources

Gifted and 2e
Defining Giftedness
http://giftedhomeschoolers.org/resources/parent-and-professional-
resources/articles/defining-giftedness/

Gifted Resources
http://giftedhomeschoolers.org/resources/gifted/

2e Resources
http://giftedhomeschoolers.org/resources/twice-exceptional/

Twice Exceptional Issues
http://giftedhomeschoolers.org/resources/parent-and-professional-
resources/articles/twice-exceptional-issues/

Overexcitabilities and the Gifted
http://sengifted.org/archives/articles/overexcitability-and-the-gifted

Parenting Resources
http://giftedhomeschoolers.org/resources/parent-resources/

Social & Emotional Issues
Living with Gifted Children
http://giftedhomeschoolers.org/resources/parent-and-professional-
resources/articles/living-gifted-children/

Davidson Resources, Social Values and Behavioral Skills
http://www.davidsongifted.org/db/browse_resources_292.aspx

Davidson Articles, Social Values and Behavioral Skills
http://www.davidsongifted.org/db/browse_articles_292.aspx

How Executive Dysfunction Can Cause Trouble Making Friends
https://www.understood.org/en/learning-attention-issues/child-learning-
disabilities/executive-functioning-issues/4-ways-executive-functioning-
issues-can-affect-your-childs-social-life

Tips for Helping Your Child Build Social Skills
https://www.understood.org/en/friends-feelings/child-social-situations

Teaching Social Skills to Young Gifted Children: Why & How

http://www.talentigniter.com/blog/teaching-social-skills-young-gifted-children-why-how

Friendship Patterns in Highly Gifted Children
http://www.davidsongifted.org/db/Articles_id_10163.aspx

The True Meaning Of Friendship
http://www.psychologytoday.com/blog/happiness-in-world/201312/the-true-meaning-friendship

Introversion in the Teen Years
http://www.psychologytoday.com/blog/the-introverts-corner/201308/introversion-and-the-teen-years

Finding and Building Community
http://giftedhomeschoolers.org/resources/local-support/

Other Great Resources
Definition of Terms
http://giftedhomeschoolers.org/resources/definitions/

Be Safe: The Movie (and resources)
http://besafethemovie.com/

Books

A 5 is Against the Law! Social Boundaries: Straight Up! An honest guide for teens and young adults, by Kari Dunn Buron

A Parent's Guide to Gifted Children, by James Webb, Janet Gore, Edward Amend and Arlene DeVries

Asperger Syndrome and Difficult Moments: Practical Solutions for Tantrums, Rage, and Meltdowns, by Brenda Smith Myles and Jack Southwick

Asperger Syndrome in Adolescence, by Liane Holliday Willey

Aspergirls: Empowering Females With Asperger Syndrome, by Rudy Simone.

Bright Not Broken: Gifted Kids, ADHD, and Autism, by Rebecca Banks and Diane M. Kennedy

Bright, Talented & Black: A Guide for Families of African American Gifted Learners, by Joy Lawson Davis

Exceptionally Gifted Children, by Miraca U. M. Gross

Gifted, Bullied, Resilient: A Brief Guide for Smart Families, by Pamela Price

Giftedness 101, by Linda Silverman

Keys to Successfully Parenting the Gifted Child, by Deborah L. Ruf, PhD and Larry A. Kuusisto, PhD

Living Independently on the Autism Spectrum: What You Need to Know to Move into a Place of Your Own, Succeed at Work, Start a Relationship, Stay Safe, and Enjoy Life as an Adult on the Autism Spectrum, by Lynne Soraya

Living with Intensity: Understanding the Sensitivity, Excitability, and Emotional Development of Gifted Children, Adolescents, and Adults, by Susan Daniels and Michael M. Piechowski

Making the Choice: When Typical School Doesn't Fit Your Atypical Child, by Corin Barsily Goodwin and Mika Gustavson, MTF

Mellow Out, They Say. If I Only Could: Intensities and Sensitivities of the Young and Bright, by Michael Piechowski

Off the Charts: Asynchrony and the Gifted Child, by the Columbus Group

Raising Your Spirited Child: A Guide for Parents Whose Child Is More Intense, Sensitive, Perceptive, Persistent, Energetic, by Mary Sheedy Kurcinka

Socially Curious, Curiously Social: A Social Thinking Guidebook for Bright Teens & Young Adults, by Michelle Garcia Winner and Pamela Crooke

Some of My Best Friends Are Books: Guiding Gifted Readers from Preschool to High School, by Judith Wynn Halsted

The Hidden Curriculum: Practical Solutions for Understanding Unstated Rules in Social Situations, by Brenda Smith Myles, Melissa L. Trautman, Ronda L. Schelvan

The Social Skills Picture Book Teaching Play, Emotion and Communication and Social Skills Picture Book for High School and Beyond, by Jed Baker

The Spotlight on 2e Series, from the publishers of 2e Newsletter

The Out-of-Sync Child: Recognizing and Coping with Sensory Processing Disorder, by Carol Stock Kranowitz

The Sensory Processing Disorder Answer Book: Practical Answers to the Top 250 Questions Parents Ask, by Tara Delaney

When the Brain Can't Hear: Unraveling the Mystery of Auditory Processing Disorder, by Teri James Bellis

For even more books and resources, check out our GHF Amazon store!

Endnotes

1. "Dabrowski's Over-excitabilities: A Layman's Explanation," *StephanieTolan.com*, Last modified March 5, 2007, http://www.stephanietolan.com/dabrowskis.htm.

2. James T. Webb, *Searching for Meaning: Idealism, Bright Minds, Disillusionment, and Hope* (Tuscon: Great Potential Press, 2013), 48-9.

3. Susan Cain, *Quiet: The Power of Introverts in a World that Can't Stop Talking* (New York: Broadway Books, 2013), 11.

4. Charles R. Martin, *Looking at Type: The Fundamentals* (Gainesville, Florida: Center for Applications of Psychological Type, 2001).

5. Ben Thomas, "Are the Brains of Introverts and Extroverts Actually Different?" *Discover Magazine: The Crux* (blog), August 27, 2103, http://blogs.discovermagazine.com/crux/2013/08/27/are-the-brains-of-introverts-and-extroverts-actually-different/#.VenWVdJ4riw.

6. Miraca U. M. Gross, "'Play Partner' or 'Sure Shelter': What gifted children look for in friendship," *The SENG Newsletter*, May 2, 2002, http://sengifted.org/archives/articles/play-partner-or-sure-shelter-what-gifted-children-look-for-in-friendship.

7. Dr. Dylan Selterman, "The 'Need to Belong'—Part of What Makes Us Human," *The Science of Relationships* (blog), April 16, 2012, http://www.scienceofrelationships.com/home/2012/4/16/the-need-to-belong-part-of-what-makes-us-human.html.

8. Selterman, "The 'Need to Belong'—Part of What Makes Us Human."

9. Selterman, "The 'Need to Belong'—Part of What Makes Us Human."

10. Judith Shulevitz, "The Lethality of Loneliness: We now know how it can ravage our body and brain," *New Republic*, May 13, 2013,

http://www.newrepublic.com/article/113176/science-loneliness-how-isolation-can-kill-you.

11. John Taylor Gatto, *Weapons of Mass Instruction: A Schoolteacher's Journey Through the Dark World of Compulsory Education* (Gabriola Island: New Society Publishers, 2010), 31.

About the Authors

Corin Barsily Goodwin is founder and Executive Director of Gifted Homeschoolers Forum. She has been publishing and presenting in the fields of giftedness, education, special needs, and parenting for over a decade. She currently resides in Washington with her husband, two teens, and three cats.

Mika Gustavson, MA, MFT, is a psychotherapist, and director of Gifted Matters, specializing in helping the gifted to thrive. She maintains a private practice and trains other professionals on issues touching on giftedness, homeschooling, and parenting. She also writes about these topics, and does her best to head up GHF's Professional Division. She works, lives, and homeschools in Silicon Valley, with her husband and teenage son, and too many knitting and crochet projects.

Made in the USA
San Bernardino, CA
09 November 2015